# SOUTHERN RANGE

## Collected Longer Poems 1980–2022

---

Ambition in contemporary poetry is often in short supply. John Lane does not suffer from a lack of ambition or a lack of skill in these extraordinary long poems. In the same way *Abandoned Quarry* shows his mastery of the short form, these poems show a poet pushing his skills while challenging his readers with a joyride of stunning imagery, amazing leaps, and sonic pleasures.

—Mike James, author of *Portable Light: Poems 1991–2021*

John Lane is one of the brightest and most versatile poets we have among us and those qualities are on ample display in this book, his venture into the world of the American Long Poem. The craft in these pieces is often brilliant, the imagery is superb, the logical structure is tight and coherent, the poems flow like mountain water. But the quality I admire most in this collection is the overwhelming sense of joy that permeates these poems. Lane's world is a world worth living in, a world where we find beauty and rapture. It is a welcome over the shoulder look back at a world we once had, a reminder of what we might find, and who we could be if we lived attentively and deliberately. I envy anyone unfamiliar with John Lane's poetry who opens this book for the first time: a grand notion awaits.

—David Lee, author of *Driving & Drinking*
and *The Porcine Canticles*

"What does poetry know?" John Lane asks. In his magnificent *Southern Range* the poet is always asking, always digging, comes close to knowing. "There's a pulse of language, / but no words. It's all narrative." With some of my own roots in Spartanburg, South Carolina, perhaps the long poem is a natural.

—Sharon Doubiago, author of *Hard Country*
and *South America Mi Hija*

## ALSO BY JOHN LANE

POETRY COLLECTIONS

*Anthropocene Blues*
*The Old Rob Poems*
*Abandoned Quarry: New & Selected Poems*
*Noble Trees* (with photographers Mark Olencki & Mark Dennis)
*Against Information and Other Poems*
*As the World Around Us Sleeps*

PROSE

*Gullies of my People*
*Coming into Animal Presence*
*Still Upright & Headed Downstream*
*Whose Woods These Are* (a novel)
*Seven Days on the Santee Delta* (with Philip Wilkinson)
*Neighborhood Hawks*
*Fate Moreland's Widow* (a novel)
*Coyote Settles the South*
*Web of Water* (with photographers Tom Blagdon, Clay Bolt, jon holloway, & Ben Geer Keys)
*My Paddle to the Sea*
*The Best of the Kudzu Telegraph*
*Begin with Rock, End with Water*
*Circling Home*
*Chattooga*
*Waste Deep in Black Water*
*Weed Time*

EDITED

*Literary Dogs & Their South Carolina Writers* (with Betsy Wakefield Teter)
*Whose Woods These Are: New Nature Writing from the South* (with Gerald Thurmond)
*Hub City Christmas* (with Betsy Wakefield Teter)
*Hub City Anthology* (with Betsy Wakefield Teter)

# SOUTHERN RANGE

## Collected Longer Poems 1980–2022

*John Lane*

MERCER UNIVERSITY PRESS
*Macon, Georgia*

MUP/ P711


Published by Mercer University Press
1501 Mercer University Drive
Macon, Georgia 31207


29 28 27 26 25 5 4 3 2 1

Books published by Mercer University Press are printed on acid-free paper that meets the requirements of the American National Standard for Information Sciences—Permanence of Paper for Printed Library Materials.

Printed and bound in the United States.

This book is set in Adobe Caslon Pro.

Cover/jacket design by Burt&Burt.

Library of Congress Cataloging-in-Publication Data
Names: Lane, John, 1954- author.
Title: Southern range : collected longer poems 1980-2022 / John Lane.
Description: Macon, Georgia : Mercer University Press, 2025. |
Identifiers: LCCN 2024054785 | ISBN 9780881460421 (paperback)
Subjects: LCGFT: Poetry.
Classification: LCC PS3562.A48442 S68 2025 | DDC 811/.54—dc23/eng/20241204 LC record available at https://lccn.loc.gov/2024054785

To D. E. Steward, for his fifty-year friendship
and his long poem, *Chroma*.

# Preface

*By Mark C. Long*

If you are like me, and hear "Southern Range" and think of the Blue Ridge mountains near John Lane's home ground, you will have a place to begin: for the longer poems collected here hang like fog on the Blue Ridge; and you will sense below the ridgelines, lurking in the draws and hollows, the tributaries of family and place—the shady streambeds, the eddies in the passing of time, the swirling waters where these poems were made.

The first poem, "From the Three Kingdoms" (1980), echoes with the emotional range and measured cadences of Theodore Roethke's *North American Sequence*,

> I dream journeys
> The world turning on my axle.
> Oaks and hemlocks above, retreating into shadow
> As a car pulls them along

as Lane sorts thoughts and memories, images and voices, confusions and delights—from childhood and adolescence as well as out of the urgent and consequential impulses that follow as we begin making our place in the world.

The mortal stakes of "From the Three Kingdoms" become visible as Lane listens in on the ever-elusive but always-indelible stories of his family and his place:

> I have been told (too young to see, too clear to remember, too
>     old to forget)
> 100 miles away
>             20 years back
>                     in late November our car coughed in the driveway
>                 as he drowned in fumes from the exhaust. (33)

Lane knows from reading one of his early poetic mentors, Ezra Pound, that the fragments of a life do not ever fully cohere; and yet this opening poem establishes the continuities ("three hundred years of family and friends") and broken ties ("*But where has my father gone?*") that swirl in the draws and hollows where "a single human history began."

Like bookends, the two poems that follow, "Against Information" (1995) and "Tweet" (2013), are reminders that individual histories are formed in relation to the vagrancies of human culture. These poems begin in a resistance to the proliferation of technology that breaks, like a fever, as Lane comes to terms with the experience of living (and writing) in the so-called information age. The sequence "Tweet" is indebted to the unfolding strophes of A. R. Ammons's *Tape for the Turn of the Year* ("parsing the idea / that information is / pollution clouds // the quality of the thinking: more is not // less. . .") in a playful homage that at the same time seizes the formal possibilities a poet will find in a digital age.

Lane's dialogue with Ammons is among this book's many delights. *In Landfill This—Five Bags of Garbage for Archie Ammons* (2014), a riff on the image that centers the book-length poem *Garbage*, Lane casts his voice into the "the great swirling Gulf Stream of poetry" (99):

> Archie, I am with you as you drive
> from Florida to Cornell and pass that smoking hulk
>
> our tomb to the Unknown Poet for an Undeclared War:
> Archie, the Forever Colossus of the Colon, filing

Here the accumulating couplets, conversational tone, and interplay of line and syntax, like Ammons, enact the process of a mind preoccupied with inexhaustible detail and surprising correspondences—the patterns we discover and then use to make meaning in our lives.

But Lane's imagination is never far from the tumbling waters of time and place—the ancient processes of the natural world and the tenuous purchase of human lives. In the prologue and twenty-one sections of the magnificent "Kingdom & Glory" (2022), Lane digs into his ancestral landscape. This haunted narrative sequence—as Lane's notes to the poem tell us, "a long, sometimes historic poem about the Pacolet River Flood of 1903"—conjures an extended parable about the lives of the people, both past and present, who inhabit his home ground.

Then, in "25 Dream Ghazals" (2022)—a poem locally sourced from a dream journal Lane has kept for forty-five years, and composed in an ancient Persian poetic form—Lane invites the reader to find in its dreamy cascade of couplets the unexpected pleasures and surprises of a poet finding his way—gathering "Facts and particulars. No softened generalities" as he strives to "Build these up the way a house rises, stud by stud." In this poem, indeed throughout *Southern Range*, Lane builds a place for shelter—perhaps even a place to call home.

MARK C. LONG, professor of English emeritus at Keene State College, is a fourth-generation Californian who lives and works on a New Hampshire farm in the Connecticut River watershed. His love for language, literature, and culture is reflected in numerous essays, book chapters, reference entries and reviews on American poetry and poetics. Mark currently serves as president of the William Carlos Williams Society.

# Contents

MERCER UNIVERSITY PRESS

*Endowed by*

TOM WATSON BROWN
*and*
THE WATSON-BROWN FOUNDATION, INC.

# From the Three Kingdoms (1980)

He was like a man who stands upon a hill above the town he has left, yet does not say "the town is near," but turns his eyes upon the distant soaring ranges.

—Thomas Wolfe *Look Homeward, Angel*

## A Prologue

From high spine of uplifted rock breaking down
Grain by grain in erosion of years of sunlight, water
Grinding mountains, the old Appalachian range
To hills and hills and hills.

From creek bottoms, from laurel draws of old creek valleys
Cut deep in broad-based hills, from eddies behind rocks
From granite rocks
Exposed by cycles of ebb, flow, flood, slow deepening
Of creek beds, from soil-creep on hillside.

From clay swirling in creeks, red silt settling
In flats, dead oak leaves riding water in autumn
Clogged in branches, winter ice
Bridging shallows, tulip poplar pollen scum
On current in spring, a dead queen snake
On a rock in summer breaking down to rot
And body-swell.

From the swell of flood, from the flow
Of soil to rivers, the thickening of bottomland
The spill and cake of mud for alders and birch
The shallow pools for cricket and chorus frogs.

From twitch and float of butterflies to birch
Wild rose, honeysuckle, thistle, heal-all, chicory,
And the buzz of blow flies, horse flies in flesh-rot
Of dead rabbit, from a moving mass of seed ticks
In deer scat, from bite and suck of the bulbed
White wood ticks on a buck's rump.

From the quick whistle of killdeer in high grass
Or a calm field rustling with quail, the reed-stripped
Neck of bittern, the scree scree of red tail hawk
In a snag, the brag of kingfisher
After catching silver and yellow sunfish.

From the blind burrow of short-tail shrew
The wolf-killed doe beside a laurel bordered stream
The black bear feast on blue berries in midsummer
The browse of elk in spring.

From these a single human history began:

1.

A green branch tics at a window, scratching
Into a glass pane. The half-steady rocking of green
Wood and wind etch unordered lines as wind shifts—

Bird paths in a beach groove.
The slick runs of worms in mud after rain.

The same green branch cut back, doused with kerosene
And lit, burning the branch, the ground around it,
Leaving ash in the black curls of grass.

This is a sign of spring, I think
And then smell the burnt ground and burnt branch,
The wind laced with the lent of blowing ash.

The green branch.

The burnt ground.

I am there.

In the common land between the two; I am living there,
Aware smoke waits in the white sponge of the stem.

All a dream, and I wake, thinking it all a senseless
Extended metaphor: Life/Death, the green branch
And the burnt ground. But now

The green branch tics at the window, in my bedroom,
Of this house, asking to become substance, me knowing
There were always trees:

First a fig tree, bulbed and sexual, the summer
I was five. Velvet leaves. This will become the texture
Of a girl's breasts, her tilted back. In summer

I staggered from bed, eyes stiff from a sweaty sleep,
And beat the heat, the birds, the insects, to catch
The green bulbs before they ripened into rich mush
Of the full fruit. But always, the grackles sat stiffly
In brown branches of the squat fig tree, waiting
For the slam of back door, the child's whirring run;
Then they scaled the still, morning air

Black users.

Plump fathers of barrenness.

Full of figs.

*There will always be trees:*
*An acorn grows an oak in its ear.*

Then once in the dead summer sun I sat under an oak
Watching heat make strange shimmers in the street.
Like the world itself had thrown off summer and healed
Itself with fever, and lost itself in another rising,
In the curved world suspended there.
Nothing held straight in those twin worlds,

One an August yard and a simmering street,
The other, a wave of bowed light; I balanced there
In the untroubled weather of childhood, leaning against
The cool bark of an oak, holding fast.

Oak. Poplar. Beech. Fig. Pine. Cedar.

How many trees can a yard hold
Before it returns to the forest? There is a house
Caught between the trees, like some remembered fairy tale,
Or an aunt's house I thought I never visited.

*Don't worry. There will always be trees.*
*The limb doesn't worry over the progress of rings.*

Once, in late summer, apple trees bowed with the weight
Of a thousand apples. I ate from the ground, picking
Worms from the white pulp, eating around brown
Bruises, filling up with softening fruit.

*Honeybees buzzed in the black decay,*
*Flies floated, slow-winged, in the festered ripeness.*

But that fall there was an undoing. There was a coming
Apart, a crack in the perfect world of childhood.
Light no longer bent perfectly over the earth;
It leaked from within, outlining my Mama between
The two trees, gathering apples.

Apple trees budded in the cracked days of April,
Blossomed in the mad, rainsoaked days of May,
Fruited in the first full bloom of August heat.

But there was an undoing in their fruiting,
In their full-bodied bulbs. My Mama's shadow
Among the fruit trees, picking through the down fruit,
Slicing the white pulp on the back porch shelf, lacing
It with yeast, sugar, filling the churns, stirring
The juice into swirling funnels of apple, capping
The churns, waiting for the second bloom of that brew.

*Down on a swirl of apple wine.*
*I found her in the kitchen.*

In the porch corner a clutch of fruit flies
Worried the air above the opened churn.
Half the cider gone, the room smelling of vinegar,

*Smelling of late summer.*
*Smelling of the thick shade of the apple trees.*

A green branch tics at this window. 4 A.M.
Thunder storm coming on, fan sucking air from the house,
Me, eating oranges, spitting seeds through two broken
Panes into late night, rain-slick grass, the sky shot
With lightning. Lightning: that leak of light,
A primeval urge to curl up, wait it out.

Mama holding her arms around my sister and me, her trunk
Sprawled across her old double bed, holding us tight
As thunder clouds. We watched the whole of the yard

Go black then blue

Black then blue
Black then blue.

*Wait it out.*
*This room going black then blue.*

A green branch tics at the window in the wind.
A shoe in the corner takes on the face of a forgotten
Uncle; my bookshelf, the faces of twenty cousins.

The windows are mouths of lost lovers

The door, a lost forest

5 A.M. No clouds. Light coming on.
Stars fading into light.

2.

*Dark in the forest.*
*Dark as time.*

The face of a leaf, the faces of so many uncles
In the enduring weather of childhood, in the dog days
Of summer, in the pipe freezing winters, I remember them:

I sat listening to the space
Between words whispered in the kitchen. My uncle
Talking my Mama down from her alcohol hell.
It's shift change.

Both of them just home from the cotton mill.
Through reams of smoke, she coughed words
Out of the packed cotton of her lungs, drank dark whiskey.

Her words were dark blossoms.
They stank with the smell of Schinley's and Viceroy smoke.
She coughed and choked on each bole and stem.
She was heavy with their packed weight.
She had stripped their field bare.
Her back ached with the weight of the heavy sack.

She dreamed trees of cotton in the yard.
She dreamed the cotton white again.

Her words were cotton; his, the dark wood of family:

"Mary you got to stop this drinking."
(she coughed the room
Full of brown cotton)
"Mary Ellen, think of the boy and Sandy."
Rattle of glass and table

"You got so much, those two kids."
Rattle of glass.

But through all the talk ran the thin thread of another
Memory: mountain drives
With six packs and chicken salad sandwiches
Cold air and my uncle driving, his voice lost in the wind,
The top down on the De Soto, my Mama's face flushed
From beer and wind.

Into the belly of the mountains.
And up            up frozen waterfalls.
Winter always winter in the clear eye
Of childhood  the clear scent
Of dead grass  decay stopped in the cedar clean
                                        air of Appalachian mountain mornings.

With my drunk Mama          drunk uncle climbing
Into east coast high country Saluda Grade air. A boy of ten,
I try to focus on something
Anything in the clear, ceaseless spray of winter wind.

Beer whizzing past
The last trunk of white oak    green hemlock
As we climb, lost in the enveloping past of just then:

*Just then Mama, did you see that tree?*

It was big as a house   big
As this uncle's beer-clouded head.

Big as Brown's Cove we just passed
That sign did say Brown's Cove
Brown your Maiden name.
Mary Ellen Brown.

Brown the right word for this day.
Brown the color of beer
Dark brown    dark as time    dark as the forest we pass.

Brown the color of sky and hills as I lie on my back
And follow a turning thread of landscape
Pulled along by one lead-footed uncle
In on dull, winter-dirtied, slow moving De Soto.

3.

Heading east over sea a blue plane caught against clouds
Clouds the color of iron
A slough of clouds
And Europe at the base of that slough:

The Atlantic basin is not a dish;
                    (The proper boy is not a dish)
It deepens with memory—first the flight.
The Atlantic basin is not to be bridged in a day;
(Old man in Washington State, while cussing bridges, said,
"If you want to cross water, paddle a canoe.")

We make it in six hours—*Wuthering Heights*, the movie—
Then take almost an hour to clear customs.
Landing in a country older than Charleston, my Paris city,
Than its Great Civil War (dishes for sale in shops, Paris
All three older than King Street).

History. Culture. Customs. Tradition. Disembodied words.
Memory holding onto only the feel of things:
Europe was a frieze of color and weather.

A fortnight touring ten countries caught
In stone before a whirring fourteen-year-old boy:

*History*

Cold in Paris standing in the rain at Notre Dame floor-grooves
A history of feet.

*Culture*

Italy, hot        but the food gave in flavor

The *Via Tiburtina*      eating at Amatrice
Hay and straw  roast baby lamb
*Vino bianco e rosso al barile*
And most of all, that stout, drunk midget stinking,
Dancing on our table kicked two plates on the floor.

*Customs*

Venice, down on a swirl of cheap wine
Drunk from the bottle offered by a Gondolier
Singing "White Christmas," the only song in English he knew.

*Tradition*

These stories passed on.

###

On the wall of my room in Virginia
                                        I have a photograph
Taken somewhere in Switzerland:
Blue mountains creased with glaciers, sharp-edged rises,

The backdrop for the portrait,

                  But in a strange twist of focus
And setting, the landscape drops off behind me,
Leaving mountains surrounding my head, my face
Caught in slight blur against a field of white.

Penciled across it in my hand:

*1970: Boy & landscape*
*Terminal Moraine*

###

The blue tour bus baked in Italian sun

Rocked through coastal mountains
Through government tunnels

Cliffs going black then blue

Cut through granite

Black then blue

Below us, the deep bowl of the bay
                                        the blue sea beyond
(Cypress growing along the pebbled shore, in the summer heat,
In the blue coast light) and Carl, the tour guide
Said, "Look, below that ridge sits the old city
Of Rapallo."

The wheels clucked on        cliff-caught
The windows went black
The cliffs went black then blue

Black then blue.

Then out of the mountains, into the narrow streets
Into the summer heat, caught between cliffs and sea.
The town in the wide windows bus windows

Italian children twisted hydrants loose fountains

Blue gutters    Standing water

Above a Piazza,
The old poet in his rocker. Morning silence
Settled around him like heat.
His blue-eyed squint made water dance below,
Go blue in spray.
A half-formed chant turned the tongue:

*I will not move I will not move*
*Blue sea / blue sky*

*The white temple cliff hung*
*The years go blue then die*

*I will not move*
*Paradise turns on a swallow's wing*
*Wind whispers the wing to sky*
*I will not move Temple turns to dust*
*Like a swallow's wing Life blazes blue*
*Then dies.*

The blue tour bus clucked through town
To our hotel into the silence I remember
That summer was Rapallo.

4.

*Horsetail. Equisetum.*
*Good for scrubbing, the Cherokee said.*

On a beer-breath morning, the cool stink of the wind
Whizzing past the car, whizzing past a stand of horsetail,
I think back through tribes of the Piedmont and Mountains:
Apalachee, Congaree, Saluda, Catawba, Cherokee.
Ah, Cherokee early spring     long past
Hunting bands walking a flat game trail along this same Pacolet
      River
In those distant east coast aboriginal times.

Now, other cars whizzing past cannot see
The flat game trail, only asphalt shimmering in sun
Only our Volkswagen parked in a pullout
Only miles and space
Road markers and Mobile maps
No history
No thrill of just then.

Just then          that Oregon Junko landed in a field of salal
On another coast        in Washington            where clouds lower
Every sky          every mountain
But I am not there
And I dream that bird up from another memory of mountains
Another year    another coast

Just then          was that our old De Soto        was that Mama
Passed out in the front seat and me
A small, fat, cowlicked boy riding the back seat
Feet up            hands out        pulling the world shut
Like a zipper as we slide past?          They're gone

*Only miles and space.*

Like a rainstorm, memory scavenges the mind clean
Leaves me caught between two worlds
The way fog settles between mountains.

I dream journeys
The world turning on my axle.
Oaks and hemlocks above, retreating into shadow
As a car pulls them along,
The silences of remembered wind and road and sun
A small boy's face lodged at the center of the universe.

Horsetail whizzes past:
I remember horsetail and I remember
The moment just before I first said the word:
In college, walking a Piedmont creekbank
Looking for snakes
David out ahead          sloshing
Slight breeze wafting back that wet jeans smell
And then, up a small high water cove the stand of
Green segmented lines almost mathematical in their long,
Leafless symmetry and flat-topped elegant vegetable stance,

Then David saw the stand and saw my puzzled stare
And said, "Horsetail. Good for scrubbing."
Horsetail.

I repeated the name, could not work out the sense
Of such a stark green skinny thing
Being called horsetail.

###

Good brother Southern poet Sidney Lanier
Died across the street from the Pacolet River
                    a stream not unlike his Chattahoochee
When it rolls out of the hills of Habersham
                            down the valleys of Hall.

Died in a two-story red brick house with a view
Of the highway, the river, the mountains behind.

Died consumptive, death-sick but maybe rapt
Finally in this good Southern air
After years in Baltimore.

Now, the cars whizz past

Someone notices the sign

But only just then

The silver square with black lettering—

"Sidney Lanier (1842-1881) Southern Poet
Died in this house."

Other cars slow, stopping for my one slowed car.
History            grinds to a halt
Horns urge it on
Good-bye brother poet
Good-bye.
I'm gone.

###

Near the highway: rhododendrons with their green
Leather leaves, sweet wet smell, the blue wheels

Of chicory    chicory    chicory
The car whizzing past
White asters  forty blooms to one stalk
And grasses slapping fenders  seeds flying
Seeds settling in the seats    finger deep on the floor
And leaves    leaves  leaves  green or red and yellow
Sometimes wet        sometimes crisp.

*Sometimes summer.*
*Sometimes fall.*

Always the blurred overburden of trees.
Hemlock and oak closing under
A scrubbed blue sky
As I climb the Saluda Grade
To reach the Hendersonville Plateau
Into the blue blue mountains into another world
Of the endless west the green rolling endless west.

5.

*for Debby*

*Sex is a sea.*
*Childhood drains steadily into*
*That deepening salty sea.*

Once in a thawing basement, early spring,
Lonnie Dawkins on top of his own blood sister
On a cold oil can lid. The boy stood in the cool shadows
Not wanting to watch, unable not to, feeling that cold sexual
Fear tingle his spine like a deer in a dead run.

He was ten, feeling the sea of sex,
stung by the sharpness of that aging.

You write from a bar in Black Mountains:
"I don't know where I'll sleep tonight. Anywhere, I suppose. Miss you."

Two years. Two years since we last felt the slow rush of sex
Beach us in every bed we took.
Outside this window a thin wire of birdsong strings the trees.
A net. A nest of hooks. Any other day I wouldn't notice
The black birds and the strained pitch of their song.
But today, it calls back, four years,
And the good love we pulled like a fine filament
Between the two poles of our lives.
Your mind was always shifting between a void
and a chaos; mine, probing that connection between.

*If sex was a sea, we swam there.*
There is too much to forget.

*There are shorelines as barren as clouds.*
There are bird prints in the beach groove.

*Listen, the sea is quiet.*
No one walks there.

*The sandpipers have left. The water is still.*
We can walk there.

Remember the tiled halls of Junior High?
When consciousness became the early apple of a girl's breasts?
There was no reality other than that:
Some padded them; this was called insincerity
Some glowed through those years in their good fortune
some let them be touched,
Not unlike moons pulling
Tides over the skin of the earth.

I still remember you: the slight sag the fullness when you stood
the settling when lying flat on your back
like no mountains
Like no moon.

More like islands.
Inland islands in some warp of time;
With the velvet texture of fig leaves

*(Warp of time)*

Now my blood warps as I think back
Re-construct
Each scene time islanded in the sea of our time together:

Once moving down a brown rooted riverbank

Away from a steel-beamed bridge
The river pulled brown moons in front of rocks brown roots
Strained the soil, bounced
In a cutbank river swash.
Birches breathed above.

A redtail hawk circled, like us, looking for snakes out in the heat
Then the sun flared through trees

We made for the bank

Ah, we warmed
Moons rose on the river the hawk screed toward home.

Time caught in a particular time
A particular place we both know like that river
Like that summer spent grinding the mountains
On the good flint of our longing
Is all we pass back and forth now.
The black bird has stopped webbing the yard with song.
Only the past remains.
Even in the dead heat of this present summer
I remember the brown thaw of early March years ago
The dry smell of the cool basement
Lonnie Dawkin's sister sinking in her own shrinking sea

*And us rising in ours.*

Wading away from a steel-beamed bridge
Ankles pin-shocked and red
Time finally slowed by cold in a river running to the sea.

6.

All flight west from this point:
Dog tired and stoned
I caught the July 5th night flight from Atlanta
To Seattle, heading west; the rest of the country
In between one great jet-age ozone blur of states

*States   states   states.*

"This is your captain, it's 51 and cloudy in Seattle.
We are now over Nebraska. To your left in the night
And distance is the Grand Canyon, Mexico, Yucatan.
Off the right-wing tip, the Canadian Rockies.
We will land sometime before the sun. Sleep,
Enjoy your flight. You have just seen America."

*Down on a swirl of travel.*

Over the northern Great Plains, that old Paleozoic swamp

Following Interstate lights through darkness
I guess is Wyoming, drunk
On the distance of that first trip west of Huntsville
Where the last of eastern forest mountains shrink behind.

Then the movie came on and I was in it—one-family,
One-cotton mill towns, drunk uncles and Burt Reynolds
Saying "Ya'll, ya'll." A woman beside me eyed
My Jack Daniels, said, "I don't drink no alcohol."

Finally, six forty-five, four hours, a whole continent
In the air, gear lowered in land, we bank out over
Puget Sound my Promised Land.

###

Open letter to a geologist *for John Harrington*

X-27-78. Port Townsend, Washington Olympic Peninsula

I'll take this slow; there's a lot of land to cover
Between here and South Carolina: from the porch
Of my small cedar and fir cabin (Doug fir, matures fast, 25 years,
Makes good framing material; cedar for siding,
Shakes for the roof) I look out over Discovery Bay.
Sighted a killer whale two days ago. Orca. It sounded
And rolled its dorsal fin across 300 yards of open
Water. The salmon, what's left of them, anyhow,
Are running now, bringing the whales in close.
On clear nights I lie out on my open porch,
Watch Arctic lights shudder through far northern skies.
When the bay clears of early evening fog (still light)
Birds drift in—gulls, mallards, coots, great blues along the edge,
Even an occasional arctic loon. A wash of particulars:
Pacific kelp clogged between driftwood fir logs washed from
Westend forest stands.

The faint glow at night.

A racoon walks the beach groove at dusk lugging a tiny sea
With him in each cell of striped-tail waddling body.

Last light a bright dream in small brains.

Coots float on darkening water bending wings, riffling feathers.

To the west and south are Olympics, spine of rock,
Sharp-edged rise of pushing continent. Close-by, the outer rim,
Further beyond that, Mount Olympus, with glaciers

Taking the mountain down. On a clear day, rare out here,
You can count the thick rivers of ice on the sides.

And everywhere: the monotonous
Green of a gone world: coniferous; reptilian.
Firs, cedar, spruce; lower in the underbrush, the ferns,
Salal, manzanita, and a few small hardwoods, alder
And maple. The hardwoods offer up the only color change
In October's first cold, reminders of the flower world
Of South Carolina—Ah... back there autumn's thousand colored
Great Smokey Mountain flurry of falling sap and chilling air:
Roads awash with yellow red yellow red green green-brown
A welling swirl of maple, birch, oak, poplar, sycamore.
When cars pass when feet kick through
Where small creeks wash out of hills
Building up an alluvium of leaves, banked there
Like sand, like the last layer of color washed
From the hills, like some great running spill and cake
Of falling foliage back there, every month leads into
Autumn, every season staged only for a last great falling
Away, that last slow shudder of color

With winter coming on

Winter working its way back east.

John, I just wanted to say
You were right—there are distances we never settle—
Like fog slung between mountains
Like glaciers taking mountains down.
I can see them from my kitchen window.

7.

*for Sam Hamill*

*The eyes seize without effort—*

Oaks above blue wheels
Of chicory, black pavement
—the mind tenses only when two plains cross:

Grey skies drag the horizon
We ride 101 down
From Asheville? from Port Townsend?

Through Olympic firs, sharp ridges
(The axle of my hand? the axle of a continent?)
Mountains wall Hood Canal sharp turns
Roll shadows
Into those black caves so many small blue water coves
Night day        night day
Creek valley rifts open landscape to sun
Slanting through fir trees        day again        hard left
Screech of tires            night again      midday.

(In a dream? in the past of just then?)
Sam rolls joints in the seat beside me
As we listen to Waylon and Jerry Jeff and Ramblin'
Jack Elliott kicking hell out of some old love song.
Any song they choose spits and smacks
On my set of low-grade K-Mart speakers
Turned up so loud and rattling, each sounds the death of music.

I left South Carolina listening to Jerry Jeff
With my Mama, her laughing and singing along,
"He's thirty-four and drinking in a honky-tonk,"
And me sitting there saying "Ma, I'm only 23."

I drew her a map of the continent, explaining
Where I was going and she kept asking,
"How far from Texas? You got people there."

"It's west Mama. Far west as I can go."
She smoked, tried to think through the distances, said,
"Johnny, you know I never been west of Asheville."

Far west of Asheville, Washington State Interstate 5—
Laid down on Pleistocene glacial flat land (game trail?)
—Taking books to the bindery.

Sam burps local Rainer beer,
Gives me a short, intense geologic history:
"East of the Cascades
                                volcanic rock lava flows Flat and black,
Spokane to mountains—shit, we're out
Of beer (beer burp beer smell) stop at that station, This exit—"
We slow into some endless stretch
Of parked trucks, gas pumps, diesel smoke. I buy beer,
We pull out toward Portland. Sam forgets the Cascades, fades back
Into some slow Sad Willie Nelson song about love or trains

Or someone bleeding, cheating crying, somewhere east of here.

Crossing the Columbia, lost only twice, we find the bindery,
Mackensie & Harris, in a low industrial
Section—bump of tracks, Sam asks, "Did you hear the one
About the man, the nearsighted man that is, who spent
The night in a warehouse?"

Inside, the clack of twenty machines,
A thousand books being bound. Sam yells—

"Most are perfect bound, cut, slap and glue. Nothing perfect in that.
Cheaper by a cent or two."

Then finally, ten workers at ten big sewing machines.
Half-joking, I ask one, "How can you read in here?"

"I don't read 'em I make em."

Then, half the dark day spent in Powell's,
Dropped 50 bucks I didn't have on books—Ditmars'
*Snakes of North America*, first edition, among them—
Sam says, "Oh hell, call it business."

And ogling Portland women on clean, downtown streets,
Wool skirts swishing in October, west coast wind—
Sam shakes his head, calls me kid.

Later on at Rhine's tavern, rounds blur.
Strange women get prettier, talk

Turns to politics and Pound—

"Wanting good government"
In their states, they first established order in their own families
(beer burp)

...and on down to precise verbal definitions and organic categories.
Beer: hops & barley & craft equals

(beer burp)

"Precisely Sam—I don't mean to cut you off,
But pass that BEER!"

*Down on a swirl*

*The eyes seize without effort.*

Blur of pitcher            blur of picture

Blur of sound into Sam's just remembered:
"Intelligence is intentional. Stupidity is national.
            Art is local."

*The eyes seize.*

Blue wheel of chicory blue wheel
Blue

8.

Green.

Green County, N.C.

Green fields

*Backed by sky, a green swirling world—*
*Dust of sand roads, diesel tractor smoke, axle grease.*

—A gone green overnight agricultural hot breezeless
Corn and beans and wheat and finally fields of fields and fields
Of broad-leafed tasseled tobacco—

Driving through that country once on mica-glinted,
Green tinted asphalt roads, I stopped at Mitchell's store, asked if anybody
Knew the Lanes. Old man, tobacco spit leaking out comers,
Bib overalls faded almost white said—

"Shit, young fella, there ain't but a Lane behind every standing tree."

"Ain't got no trees in this farming country,"
I shot back, cracked him up.

I drank a coke, turned down six smokes, when they found out
I'm John's boy. "We see the favor," they say, "John had eyes like yours,
All deep and dark, but ready to crack
A good downhome country joke."
Standing in that store I felt some connection of kin
Going deeper than genes or marriage—

*Place or proximity.*

—Old coke drinking flatland fanners chewing, coughing, cussing
Not caring that I live on the road.

My parts made that way by three hundred years of family and friends
Making flat cleared fields say tobacco    corn    beans.

*But where has my father gone?*

Among the old men talking in the store.

*I didn't see him.*

"He has taken the car. He will be back.
The night isn't black enough to hold him away.
He has gone to the car."

*I remember*

A photo, circa 1954. My father stands beside
A small boat    fishing hat pushed back
Work clothes the lake tight as a drum behind him—
But that was before the camera struck it, sending out
Shimmers seen only at the picture's edges        and where
The film's        memory            strikes his eyes
And small circles of pain follow out
From every point. His pupils are the black
Still centers of the photo.
After the camera caught him, he goes on
With what he was doing or is doing,
Cranks the boat onto the trailer
Or puts it in to fish,
Worrying the air, the lake's surface
With his presence.

*Show me where my father has gone.*

He is gone

*From the seat beside my Mama as we drive.*

The steep grade to the mountains through the green shade
Through the dry cedar smell through the beer smell of faceless uncles.
At ten I don't miss him, five years gone.

All the aunts and cousins say, "We'll go to his grave."

A small military marker. Dogwoods blossoming in the late spring.
The headstone and footstone
An alien stone bought for a death marker.

(Early Indian coastal tribes traded shells and soft sediment rocks for
The hard glint of granite— good for tools, good for hammers.

The marker is Granite
Of place        100 miles east.
Bought for a marking stone planted among the dogwoods,

*Is my father in his place?*

(I too young to see, too clear to remember, too old to forget)
100 miles away
                    20 years back
                                        in late November our car coughed in
    the driveway
      as he drowned in fumes from the exhaust.

*(Yams sweetened in the stiffening ground.)*

The cough of the car.
I slept in the green glow

Of a night light.
He slept in the white stillness of midnight.

*I have found his place.*

Father. Son.     Circle. To start with the center.
My rock settles into this farm pond's water. Two more.
Now the last wave lipping cow-stand bank.

"To measure a circle you start with any point."

A point. This pond, this cow-stand.
Mud sucked up in hoof holes, caking cuffs of my jeans.

He came here too; watched
Cows cool hours under gnawed oaks, listening to this
Same sound pulled from this coastal North Carolina
Stock pond with a stone.

He died before we squatted here together.
Now cows rump bare oaks in thick shade. I sit here, smell it all:
Mud, cows, hot sun on dry grass:

Father, son, circle
It all goes on.

9.

Like a rainstorm, memory scavenges.
Leaves me caught between two worlds
The mind clean

*The way fog settles between mountains.*

I dream journeys.
Oaks and hemlocks retreating into shadow beer breath
The world turning on my axle, one world moving
Away under me through the silence of remembered
Wind and road and sun,
A spinning world caught at the center of a universe.

Another world consists of a settling,
Finding freedom has nothing to do with motion

Instead longs for steady repetitions:

Two weeks at the same beach every summer
Amid half-years in rented houses in Spartanburg,
Never long enough to see my best friend outgrow his Sunday suit
The one I might get in hand-me-downs.

Those Augusts back then fog settled on the sea leaving the sea dark.
Early morning before direct sun
                                        burned fog away Mama walked there
Carried the sun's own darkness in her then sober
Face, as if healed by the sea's own salt and wind.

As a child I watched from the cottage
Porch as she disappeared into fog
Appearing again later   changed over

In pitch with the sea's sanity.

# Against Information (1995)

The Age demanded...

—Ezra Pound

## I. New Satellite Dishes

*Today the next satellite dish is announced,*
*"pizza-sized," 18 inches across, pulls in*
*150 channels, mounts on roof top, railing,*
*window seal, $699.95, includes decoder box*
*and remote control.*

This is the latest machinery. This is the council of technicians.
User friendly. Installs in minutes. No adjustments necessary.
Lifetime guarantee. Call now for a free demonstration.
1-800-555-dish. The greatest innovation since the tractor.
Get rid of the old dish in your yard. Plant seedlings in it.
You out there in Iowa, feed your hogs from the bowl. In California,
fill it with water for a pool, or put it in the barn, in the attic
like your grandmother's hat box.

The old dish is the Olduvai Gorge of past entertainment,
the last empire charged on your credit card, the Hindenburg
of information, the Pony Express of movies, the siege
catapult of sports. This is the Age of Information
and smaller machinery clears all misunderstandings about
who won the Series, the latest theories on evolution,
the number of American medals at the Olympics, the sexual
orientation of Michael Jackson, and who is president.
Right now someone is mounting the new pizza dish,
somewhere else there is an English muffin dish, a silver
dollar dish, a dish the size of a penny. And next
to the easy chair rests a new decoder with 500 channels.

And from the glowing screen somewhere a man speaks
in a hundred voices about the coming of Christ,
another of the Serengeti, another of measles
and the Home Pharmacy. Don't open your hearts to "Car Talk."

Fall on your knees for diversity. Don't punch from AM
to FM. The pale hand taps a remote, the circuits
respond like Lipizzaner stallions. In Sarajevo the radio
broadcasts men walking through snow. The signal bounces
off cloud cover and huddles like rats in the condensers.

On cable a former beauty queen adjusts her makeup, airtime
moments away, the satellites poised above, the recoilless
rifles asleep in caves in the hillside. The howitzers
trundling over ruts to the rear. The beauty queen's
waist is thin as a mortar shell. Her technician counts
to ten backwards as the satellite pivots in space.

Welcome to the war. Welcome to the future. Welcome
all of you out there in Iowa who have just tuned in.
I lift a signal from one of the former garden spots.
I stand here lighter than the year I won the title.
I laugh when it is appropriate. I bleed when called.
My blond hair is styled in the midst of war and rape.
My finger nails are not broken. I'd eat three squares
if not dieting. I'd fly to Paris to diddle my boyfriend.
I'd drink water hauled in by jet from some other world.

## II. Resumes for Poets

*Yesterday in the mail a friend sends ten resumes*
*of poets, dense, endless lists of publications,*
*jobs and education.*

The slow drift of lives across paper, the black ink
of ambition, the alphabetical staircase of greed,
the pedigree of corruption, hand-to-hand, the buddy,
the crony, the slap-my-back-I'll-slap-yours
network we need for hiring. The pages
more real than a body. The trespass of image
and the urban sympathy of committees. The trees
cut down and processed. The trucks. The diesel fuel.
The chain saws. The dry rot. The loam. The earthworms
uprooted and listed under education. The pine
warblers cited like foundation grants. The Guggenheim
of endless streams running muddy with silt. The NEA's
fire break channeling obscenity past careers and money.
The white space, speaking of institutional loneliness,
and dark type screaming the rage of tenured fathers.

Fed Ex all resumes back to their organic source!
Reconstitute the forests. Cancel all poetry classes
and workshops! Two douglas fir for the Iowa workshop!
A loblolly and slash pine for the Johns Hopkins seminars!
Eight western cedar and a manzanita for the low residency
MFAs! I am the new prophet of a pulpless ambition!
I am the last photo copier to blindly collate
multiple submissions! I am the last poem published
in *The New Yorker* and listed for hire! My resume empties
itself monthly! Each week I exhaust the need
for another entry under publications! I drain

the sap back to the trunk! I worry the toner
into multiple components unusable by me!
I do not staple, fold, or crimp the corner!
I do not stand in line for return postage!

## III. More Memory

"Apple announces the Super Mac with super
memory..."
—*AP News* Item

I announce the digital machine's memory is a meddling list.
The file server hums as it runs on the electric current
of time. The file server spins on days and days, indexing
the past, present and future. Everything fits, everything
in alphabetical order, scanned for virus, displayed
in 640 colors on the screen. I announce the first computer
invective that doesn't scan for virus. I announce lessening
all memory. I announce forgetting. This poem is breathing,
without virtual memory, without Windows. When this poem
becomes a computer it will run no DOS, with RAM headed
in the wrong direction, with duel floppies, no hard drive,
a dot matrix printer, with software still at the 1.0 level.

This is the ancient software update of what if:
What if the silicon drained back to the white beach?
What if the waves washed grooves in all microchips?
What if computers could be lodged in the hinge of an oyster?
What if the apple rotted and the worms of pencils crawled
though the flesh? Then I would type my name with
the syllables of breath. Then I would feel dirt under
my finger tips, my prints new as a software update.
Then I would reinhabit Plato's cave, and Heidegger's
schoolhouse. Then I would stand with Wordsworth in the glen.
This day I announce the software of syllabics, dactyls,
spondees and iambics like keys on a keyboard. I announce
the hard dive of tradition, the RAM of books, the program
of handwriting, a code to be broken anew, memory of book

stores, the mother board of a comfortable chair, silence
and time. The virtual reality of a walk in the woods.
The workshop of hands on a chest. The laptop of scattered
love. The modem of desire. The e-mail of old letters.

## IV. Order

> "Simple events give rise to complex systems
> and complex events give rise to simple results."
>
> —*a physics* CD-ROM

Rising in the distance is a complex mountain range.
    Rising nearby is a garden in springtime.
    Rising from my desk is a simple mote of dust.
    Rising tomorrow is a sun I'd call possibility.
    Rising water is a sign of heavy rain.

Rain is the seasonal sign of patterns we call weather.
    Weather is infinite sadness when connected to love.
    Blue days are memories of solitude.
    Solitude is the last refuge of endangered grief.
    Rising always behind us is the memory of childhood.

Forgetting is like a child's wagon or the programming
    on a channel with bad reception. A reception
    is not always the place to offer invective like this.
    I am like a computer indexing a long manuscript,
    running all night in the professor's office,
    the words falling into place like rain in a puddle.
    And what of the order of sadness, the order of unknowing?
    The mind follows thought through one course until
    it rests like the anthropologist tracking the ape
    through a day in the treetops. She looks at her journal,
    traces each impulse back to the source, order today,
    order tomorrow, order when the sun rises and sets.

Order today for a special offer. Order today and get the power
of complexity and chaos. Order today for the knives of blood
and intuition. Order today for the multimedia of Picasso,
Blake and Jung. Order today for the printing press.
Order today and I'll ship Second Day Air. Turn quickly to
the page of your absolute longing. Get out your beads
for trade. Order today.

## V. Certainty

> "Sooner murder an infant in its cradle than
> nurse unacted desires."
>
> —*William Blake*

I have rewritten the Bill of Dreams in the left ventricle
of the human heart. I have etched a new compact there
with a laser finer than sunlight. I have spelled
all the words with exploding vowels to enrich the blood
for travel and uncertainty. I have set the heart in motion
again after this major surgery. I have floated
the last college student's unacted desire to the level
of dogma. I have posted all jobs on speculation, even
the jobs reserved for the soul-hungry. I reconstitute
the Underclass of Waking Dreams. I assemble the young
lonely lost men without Master Cards or Money Markets
reserved in their names upon graduation. I rent
and never own. I drive an old truck, paid for in the 50s
by an Indian in Nevada with no belt and a bad hangover.

There was never a logic of career. There was only the seed,
always subject to weather. There were always graphs,
job listings, quotas, and the market. But there was
always behind the abstractions a field called chance,
a range of hills where you could lose the present.

This we call finding your way in our language.
This we call the wandering among opposites, the old
clanging rocks, the journey, the search, the pilgrimage,
the walk-about, and this we endorse over the perfect resume,
a suit and tie, a second interview, a free business lunch.

I reject all economic metaphors but return. I reject bottom
line, profit, short and long run, interest but not return;
I reject dividend, currency, liquid assets, bankruptcy,
GNP, the stock market, standard of living, the check out
counter, but not return; I reject change, progress, money,
production, packaging, buying and selling, worth,
economics, territory, democracy, education. I maintain
return, and in the place of all other choices I slip
the pulse of the heart, the implicating wind, mystery
of origin, the timid choice that leads to bounty,
the bountiful rejection in the face of ages of logic,
soft collars, soft sell, wet nest, the timid voice,
resumes not postmarked in time for the grand prize,
timeless needs like desire.

Now I return to certainty: the paths beaten dusty by years
of fearful travel, blackberries picked nearest the road,
the easy ten pounds lost to the latest diet, books long
on the best seller list about what men fear, reading
assignments with no teeth, tests in fraternity files,
Friday night parties and the hangovers that follow.
I return like Blake to desire. I return to the impulse
of personal knowing. I return to the escape from parents
and elders. I return to Oedipus and his mother.
I postpone the complex, and embrace the dark.
I don't write away for more information. I take
a job in a restaurant and own one suit of clothes.
I wait on tables and make love late in the morning.
I don't see my life closing in at thirty. I don't

respond to requests for money from my alma mater.
I return my parent's calls, but melt down the extra
key. I own an impractical dog, a grey hound
in trauma from racing. I know people on drugs in spite
of the war. My opinions are revolting to textile
interns. My draft card has been washed. I believe
in a cash economy and worship folding money.
I quote China as a model for simplicity.

And for desire? The blood in any muscle. What dries first
in a child. What is easily lost sight of in the storm
of allegiances like college and family. Future pulsing
the present if you listen for the slurring sound
in the chest. It is mistakes and surprises.
Not the implicated step or the path with handrail.
Always turns in a padded swivel. It is what hinges before
the rust sets out to close the mechanical gap.
Desire is the hydraulics of deep need. Desire is the only
channel open of silt, the only canal open to the one alone.
It is Blake's original and only essential crime
and it is mine.

# Tweet (2013)

"if i
should tell you anything"
(that eagerly sweet caroling
self answers me)
"i could not sing"

—e. e. cummings

1.

most information
is garbage
our equivalent

of coal smoke
belched atmosphere
by 19th Century

factories
by buskers
of industry

by diesel trains,
consumers
in busses, cars,

fleets of trucks,
coal plants
we cook this soup

daily drifts
numbers climb
big data

100,000 tweets
per minute
as we cook

1.1 billion
Facebook users
two million

Google searches
in 60 seconds
it took to read

this skinny
column of words
#whocooksforyou

the owl cries
the talk show host
asks downloaded

from Youtube
(365,000 views)
asks the author

of a best-selling book
on nearby food sheds
and buying local

purchased on Kindle
a code processed
automated shipped out

in the dark night
the fence of sycamores
is like a screen

saver of shadows
on the yard's edge
the big moon no comfort

the owl hunting
or courting
on the temporal edge

we cook up
conceits based
on old relationships

predatory lending
captains of industry
Farmville .99 cents

brightly colored
in the App Store
CityVille free

when outside
the barred owl
hunts and calls

the next Happy Meal
somewhere below
in the rotting duff

2.

next day
pin ball dawn
Pac-Man sounds

bird talk soup
call it a kitchen full
of sharp knives

clear vowels, a crow's
#caw-caw-caw
does this chef of loss

hold the latest
numbers on songs
intended

to be hummed
only once more
to the calypso beat

of Oblivia, a tropical
country full of
tasty noisy birds?

I'm reading too
much E. O. Wilson
on extinction

the good Dr. believes
in the ark called
conservation

(send in your donation

on-line
or the gig is up)

I believe
in attention
this morning

but know what's
missing out there
is all that's

come before
mothballs
keep the mice out

of specimen drawers
pulled one by one
into the lab light

can we buy any
miracle hear
the missing song?

there is a record
of what's still here
many species

a bird App
(expensive, $9.99)
avian language

a connection
through mnemonics
song traded in

#coveritup
#cover it up
inside this

chorus
a feathered poetry
a creeping up

language's tree
backward
like the nuthatch

3.

parsing the idea
that information is
pollution clouds

the quality
of the thinking:
more is not

less, in a mind-
sense, and just
because tapping

the screen summons
an infinity of
applications

memory stored
in the tablet's
dark corners

or even purchased
and pulled
from the sky (or

some
metaphorically
named

approximate storage
off-device) is not
defensible in

a universe of confirmed
finite resources:
I know I'm on

thawing tundra
but I mean
concrete resources

in the ground
and confirmed
by geologists

(that's so
19th century)
anointed by standing

committees of peers
you wouldn't
look to chiropractors

would you to
read those core
samples of Greenland:

so why attend to
140-character
thumb-jokeys

who think whatever
they ship out
to the wired universe

on an application
now more ubiquitous
than newspapers

should be gospel?
if there is
tweeting to be

done, let the birds
do it, that is
unless the poem

moves so far
(and so quickly)
away from language

toward music
that common sense
is lost and notes

become like
digits in a complex
equation:

I enter this
poem daily
but mostly

I'm fixated
on where bird song
seeps in, not

on the history
of technology and my
past poetic discontents:

mocking bird
you have no mnemon
Tower of Babel

Whitman's musical
shuttle, Coltrane's
sheets of sound

a rope of notes
repeated as dawn
clears the near oaks

#tea-kettle
#tea-kettle
#tea-kettle

the Carolina wren
sails the day's
opening archipelago

the cardinal's comments
#cheer-cheer-cheer
#purdy-purdy-purdy

there is no outside this
feathered council
at 6 A.M. the door open

4.

my iPhone
makes the same
sounds repeated

so real the titmice
in threes and fours
swarm the feeder

which is larger
the chorus of dawn
or the digital web

open with a key stroke
the whole earth
or the earth recorded?

#tweets
bird sounds
no, bird songs

out my open door
but also the cultural
utterance

Ammons' "image
that withstands
multiplicity"

the ambient
image
the giving

of self
to governing
songs

5.

in the old spiritual
the image of the infinite
yet particular sparrows

one large eye
on them all, millions
a brown God-tended

tide flowing in daily
from the river's edge
in twos and threes

whose bull's eye isn't
on the birds
they sing, though some

wouldn't call it song
a blundering line
of slurred sharp notes

#chiddik
#chiddik
#chiddik

sparrows cavort
patrol the gravel
doing honest battle

with smaller tribes
of pigeons and even
one mild robin

built for this city's
 sycamore shade
 with compact burnished

bodies and white fluting
on tails and long primaries
I love survival in spite

of what we do to what
they had, partners now
in a city covenant

New York
a city if any
building information

a commodity
the digital screens
over Time Square

transposing
figure and ground

the image pixels
so far up they
form a girl's face

or is the screen's
meaning merely
look up, worship?

6.

The rock dove
#Coo-coo
alone on carpet

in the US Air
terminal
La Guardia

where else
makes a living
off gate food

a middle class
existence
in the bird world

7.

the latch of language slides
I listen but can't sing
the bald-faced cardinal

circles the feeder
flies to near-wood
the tangle sprung

by active verbs
like switchblades
in the branches

8.

the thrush cries
#Pyrenees, Pyrenees
the long days build

and rise beneath
a sky the color
of blue jay wings

9.

resident
grackles
inky as

Poe's raven
disassemble
the leaves

their beaks
tick and needle deep
in the decaying

wind-fall
they gather
shrill calls

#clack
#clack
#clack

through
the ragged
rigging of oaks

acorns knocked
loose rattle
the tin roof

10.

when
nighthawks hunt
the windy evening

they make two sounds
one cruising
#pee-eet

and one when
they dive to earth
#beeeer

11.

#wooooo
this owl is death
dear friend

or is it just
a hungry bird
in dark woods

12.

hunt the margins
of the onscreen app
as if a baited field

bird names rise
like real doves
from the pages

hawks, their habits
silhouettes, and cries
look for animal tracks

formed like letters
the great blue heron is easy
so much like writing

13.

the red-shouldered
hawk focuses
vision's hot spots

double fovea
painting
on the retina

my image
#ke-yer
#ke-yer

retreats through
rough branches
into deep woods

Tennyson's
watcher
is more than verse

in these
wet woods
all year

our breeding pair
resident
noisy raptors

I once told students
the right image
clarifies

grounds

abstractions
in the concrete

but the hawk's
yellow eye
composes

my surprise presence
cast there
nothing satisfying

sudden light
arranged for action
in immediate space

14.

goldfinch
does your piano
have more keys

or is that
long and moderate
warble

#pa-chip-chip-chip
#pa-chica-ree
or finally #potatochip

a flightcall
notes fried in fat
the yard's junk food

15.

a drum
heavy rain
and bird song

a downpour
like gravel
on a tanned hide

the cardinals
return first
even the male

with no feathers
from the neck up
like a leather hood

pulled tight
over a tiny skull
then crow arrives

the same
dark bald skull cap
as if the yard

is invaded
by a tiny tribe
of medieval executioners

they stash
their little axes
in the trees

16.

then the cardinal
foraging all summer
in scarlet robes

gathered tight
at his barren black neck
once he offers communion

a fledgling on the rail
shakes gray gown
her immature wings

in a ceremony of thanks
the black-oiled sunflower
seed stripped of its hull

17.

pileated woodpecker
#kik-kik-kik-kik-kik
raids the suet cage

Lord God Bird
at a distance
in the trees

feathered
sledgehammer
on my feeder

18.

a friend
writes of blue birds
on her lawn

I joke happiness
landed
#pew-mew

(sharply
the field guide
advises)

I practice
on the dog
untroubled

beside me
a failed
vocalization

one species
calling to two
with no return

why can't
I live a feathered
life, tiny heart

brief happiness
sometimes
only a season

but even
bluebird
Methuselah

gets five years
must seem
a great plain

stretching
unbroken
but there is

a life that
comes of being
our feathered joy

19.

this radiance
all life
winged life

crawling life
the mealy-mouthed
earthworm

yesterday
in the herb bed
foraging

the first mourning
dove calling
#hoo-ah-hoo-hoo-hoo

truisms
castings
like cell calls

deleted posts
discarded hard drives
Bernoulli cartridges

zips
floppy disks
typed pages

written notes
scratchings
cuneiforms

glyphs
graphs
on temples

even more
ancient
cave walls

casings
of our desire
guano droppings

deposits
twitter
in the yard

20.

#I'm pleased,
pleased, pleased
to meet ya!

the chestnut-
sided warbler
whistles at

us, the passing
bikers, on
the Creeper Trail

a perfect tourist
greeter for a
second-growth

industry (logging
then bike-riding)
these warblers

prosper in
"thickets, briars,
and bushy lands"

birds like us
thrive and wane
and some fade away—

the ivory bill, passenger
pigeon, Carolina
parakeet, to name

three once numerous
in these high places
the bike-seat philosopher

with plenty of time
rolling downhill
for 17 miles

when not humming
*Petticoat Junction*
thinks of the patterns

of habitat/extinction
species expansion
pleased, pleased

to meet ya
old-growth
naturalist

John James
Audubon
you only saw

one chestnut-sided
in old-growth rambles
(no bike only pony

and tireless feet)
so take that
I've seen
ten so far
Jimmy Boy
as we descend

to Damascus
"extinction is 4-ever"
the bumper sticker

I saw in the outfitter's
parking lot
but so far the little

bird has beat the odds
and works this
second-growth

forest like a logger
but I know
extinction is

a last paycheck
a drained account
bills unpaid

and larger trees
and fewer briars
and damn you're gone

like log trucks
and spur lines
and iron mining

we all face it even
clever tourists
bombing down

from Whitetop
on precision
recreational

machines
rented
for the day

21.

What bird sings
#aroraborealis
travel weary

on the descent
to Crabtree Falls
I hear in

dead hemlocks
the Neil Young
lyric over and over

think at first
It's from his
Cortez song

appropriate
enough in hemlocks
lost to conquest

by white aphid
but what bird
whistles Neil

Young? water
ousel maybe
or yellow-eyed

vireo at the
bottom of
the waterfall

three boys
search for service
on iPhones

wait for parents
left behind
up top

22.

standing
on the porch
I saw

the luna moth
chased by
the female cardinal

through the rainy
backyard
like a WWI dogfight

how close
she came
to insect oblivion

is debatable
and I'll never know
where the persimmon

green leaves spent
the dreary day
tucked away or dead

23.

does the hooded
warbler think
“two in the bush”

the tiny
bird hitching
a surprise ride

#djoueat, djou eat
djou eat this year
the song unsung

until the bird
flew out the open
car window

and onto
my friend’s
Facebook feed

24.

it's not like
the knowledge
isn't there

find it, sort it
shaft out of ignorance
cold stone to hot

lava, the grass tip
growing upward
and the field guide

gone to print
gone to market
gone to moldy

memory on somebody's
shaded study shelf
the rare folios

the vexed shifting
subjects like ranges
or taxonomy

the names and nuances
the bird calls
the born-again

ornithologists
on stand-by
at urban airports

the flight to Arkansas
and at the destination
repeated canoe outings

deep into some thicket
where at any moment
(like Paul on the road)

bird call
avian thrum
could break into revelation

or bogus whistle
or knocking on trees
like no other on

recording devices
a sound thought gone
now rescinded

from oblivion
by hope
Hieronymus Bosch

couldn't paint
a better scenario
bass boats

Billy Bobs
dudes straight
out of Duck Dynasty

escorting PhDs in waders
and L. L. Bean coveralls
eating the pancake special

at the Ivorybill Inn
$4.25 with tip
a gone bird

a long shot
in the hot temple
of academic desire

a common bird
looked over in the yard
what is that swing

that bird strings
five notes between
I know crow and I

know Carolina wren
but that one
will I never know

species vanish
sometimes it's
so-called "natural"

and sometimes it's
a hell of a screw-up
like the next Wal-Mart

or wood tracts
for sewing machines
or a highway pushed

through wetlands
to the last resort
woods that forged

God's big hammer
gone to stump fields
and dried black powder

oh lost, the poet
might say
or oh found

sings the fire ant
whitetail, turkey,
hog, and coyote

the exposed edges
of rich-in-possibility
if you're wired that way

25.

my brain
just lit out for
the territories

as Mark Twain
might say
the only thing

that will float
my raft
is the risky

past-time
(our national)
of improvisation

diverted for
an instant
what bird cries

#Huckleberry
#Huckleberry
#Huckleberry

or is it
#semi-pro
#semi-pro

#semi-pro
the last syllable
rising like

a gas bubble
burped
from the Ice

Age before
the last
(does a glacier

have heart-
burn, or heat
burn?) we're all

at risk in this
contracting
avian bloom

we call for now
the Holocene
at least until

the geologists
meet in 2016
and vote

on a new eon
the Anthropocene
named for you

know who
us, us
the Big Cheese

but how much
bigger actually
is our so-called

special heart
than an ostrich's
and our so-called

special needs
than the just
arrived downy

woodpecker
#whatbill?
#what bill?

(the blue
shafted cheap-
skate cries

#pick-it-up
#pick-it up)
who prefers

the suet feeder
to seeds
in a plastic tube

but diverted
back to the idea
of a die-off

—that's not like
the one cast
in machine shops

how anthropocentric
can I get
in my so-called

special metaphors
#crackmeup
#crack me up

hey, isn't this
a nature poem
so stick to birds

like right now
back to the
empty suet cage

like the empty
mind of the classic
Asian monk

or the maw
the crevasse
in the glacier's

diminishing face
or my noodle
perplexed by bird song

26.

144 "Canadian"
geese (4 more than
a tweet)

euthanized
you know
#honk-honk

in Dallas, NC
a public park
not for the birds

a "health hazard"
(too many quotation
marks around

words and clauses
in parenthesis
smell like

clever
professors
of the humanities)

and can fowl
(sorry for the pun)
a skinny column

of words
fast as goose shit
on a jogging trails

27.

this one
is for the birds
but they sure

don't care
I read stanzas
stair stepping

downward
out loud every
morning

(laugh at my own
jokes, struggle
with how

to show line
breaks—my
voice rising)

hey out
there, Big Avian
World

this is poetry
culture's seed pod
calories

to burn
but no one
especially the birds

wants to hear
a whining poet
(tweet, tweet)

28.

a feathered
kinship
back to dinosaurs

(how long did
you think I'd hold
off without bringing

them in) tiny
pastel colored
reptiles

occupying
niches filled
now by robins

what a hoot
the stretch of time
between them

and now, eons
who cares
out there

where the
descendants
scurry

among leaves
they leave me
rifting, bird

to bird
ground-feeders
#coo-coo

dove bog
cacciatore
chicken wings

.99 cents
for ten
at Bojangles

they eat
the world
worms beware

why not we
take-out ordered
from above

bull bat
bald eagle
chicken hawk

29.

I admit narrative
is not my strong
suit, nor punctation

both those
up this chimney
like smoke

or swallows
like we see downtown
circling funnels

parabolas
pulsing vortexes
out of abandoned

chimneys
still black with soot
(a winged geometry

a spiral jetty
spinning jenny
no sound surrounding)

all that motion
and not even
a simple #peet

imagination
is like those birds
passing over

I know the world's
intricate musings
only as sketched

across the night
sky in black and white
no color or contrast

if you look up
and see them leave
the black depths

count yourself lucky
among the inquisitive
among the less deciphered

30.

The glass pane
birds find it
all around

we hear them
slam
broken necks

the way out
is not always
through

35.

these private
tweets
the bouncing

multiple
morning notes
the way

cries harness
all attention
to the trees

some clicking
in the leaves
beyond pattern

I am in sympathy
with a distant
little green heron

at the creek
hours before
I hear its

repeated #skews
but I do not cruise
out among the notes

I stay here
keys tapping
tapping pause

tap again
crews of titmice
(is it plural?)

have moved
on the feeder
their white droppings

cover the railing
each one hammers
a black oil seed

until the husk
shatters
some fly close-by

(the yaupon holly
a favorite
for the spiny

foliage)
and anvil on
the tan bark

until a cleaving
seam opens
#Peter, Peter

Peter, cries
the foreman
of this harvest

(if I may be so
anthropomorphic)
this is no factory

though, the little
bird more John Henry
than Peter

or miner, gray
smock and orange
vest, if anything

the seed tube
a deep shaft
into our species'

prosperity
that's what
I want to say

here clearly
this spackle
of words

would not
diminish their
being here

feeding
we are no better
or worse for

our so-called
success and failure
than the birds

of the field
like Jesus said
only reversed

the sparrow's
eye is on us
and we are but

one among many
(constantly diminishing forms)
feeding entities

# Landfill This—Five Bags of Garbage for Archie Ammons (2014)

We can write poems that disintegrate before the reader's eyes.

—A. R. Ammons

## Bag 1.

The center slips away, each search, or was there ever
a center to start with? Photos stored off-site, "in the cloud"

as they say (and let me tell you, there are enough
clouds to go around these days), no hold, or holds, barred

in the fist fight they call a digital culture, like those photos
on Facebook you wish to disappear they're somewhere

in a million Google data servers (centers?) worldwide
using 220 megawatts of power, that's mega-fleets

of servers, sometimes as many as ten million computers
connection-to-connection, to power up for all those searches

by possible or nosy current employers (what were you thinking:
shirt off, beer pong, shit-faced?): why search unless something

is really lost, and what is, that is the question, begs all
those useless trivia answers, conundrums, cacophonies

information feeding our brains, fogging the windshield
of what matters: like the death (like death) on the Chattooga

a rafting tourist fallen out at Jawbone, swept in high water
(all this rain) into Sock-em-Dog, the body snagged somewhere

in the real maelstrom, or the dead woman on the Potomac
swept from her kayak below Great Falls, or the other

tourist in Swimmers Rapid on the Youghiogheny
his leg caught in a discarded throw rope, (ironically

called a "safety rope" by one report), the stories moving
on Google, one search after another: they're all three

dead, no matter how much living remains in currents
of ones and zeros moving server-to-server, posted

on Facebook, pictures, tributes, video shot weeks before
(so funny then, so painful to watch now) of her running

a waterfall, the view count heading toward viral
when she's dead: there are ghosts we all see, the shadows

just out the corner of the eye, fog moving in our valley
where there is no fog, but these digital ghosts don't go away,

(at least until the solar flare or the half-mile wide asteroid
predicted by a panel of experts on The Weather Channel)

web pages left up, abandoned like the BI-LO grocery,
the roof collapsed and the windows like eyes thumbed shut:

the messages piled up in Gmail, comments, numbers still live
(for dead people) on Skype, these will never compost,

like discarded beer koozies in a black plastic bag,
our digital life built up toward heaven in its ghost mound

## Bag 2.

When a tree falls in the forest, forget that old
saw about whether it makes a sound if there's no

one there to hear it crash, ask instead how old it is,
and how long it will take to rot: they say a year's rot

for every one photosynthesizing, (remember from freshman
biology, the process where oxygen and carbon cycles

are closely related and intersect, where the energy of sunlight
transforms water plus atmospheric carbon dioxide into

carbohydrates, read sugar, and builds rings of rich wood
breaking down over time, what we call rot, or decomposition,

or its study, *taphonomy* from the Greek word *taphos*, "tomb"):
anyway, RIP A. R. Ammons, fallen father oak, rotting 12 years,

unless, that is, the poet wasn't cremated, or shot full of chemicals
and sunk like a common corpse in some mausoleum or crypt:

but sometimes cremation doesn't do it, especially with poets,
the others, not the scientists, Percy Shelley's heart wouldn't

burn (with Lord Byron looking on) after he drowned in 1822:
I'm not telling you anything you don't know if you've read

*The Oxford Book of Literary Anecdotes*, a text full of slowly
rotting literary trees ironically enough entombed in a book

made of wood pulp soon rotting itself on some shelf or in
some landfill (the proper climate control to keep paper

viable is both expensive and rare): and what of poems as
opposed to anecdotes (from the Greek *anekdota*, "unpublished"):

how are we to gauge a poem's afterlives and when, even,
are they dead? We know poems do not die with the poet

or the poet's family, no matter how hard they try to lock
them up in the tomb of the literary estate (a few dollars for

a Frost poem, a fortune for one of T. S. Eliot's), though sometimes
a poem is stillborn and never lives, like an oak spout burned

in the season's last frost, green and living for a moment, but
quickly God's mulch, a sip of nutrient for some recycler,

reduced to a swirl of slime in the Duff's salad bar for
worms, flies, beetles, and aphids: and you, Archie, your poem

seeds planted and grown to timber, still crisp as iceberg lettuce
as I read this summer from your *Garbage:* your heart did not

burn, but rots slowly in libraries all over, a forest of words:
but if I burned *Garbage* on the beach, the book washed ashore

shipwrecked out of the great swirling Gulf Stream of poetry
the storm of publication, reviews, prizes, biographical

footnotes, annotations by critics: what would remain but
a rusting pile of semi-colons burnished by wind and rain?

like black BBS, salvaged punctuation, a pyramid of scrap metal
ball bearings, or the eyes of cartoon characters unlinked and

rolling on the pavement: Archie, I am with you as you drive
from Florida to Cornell and pass that smoking hulk

our tomb to the Unknown Poet for an Undeclared War:
Archie, the Forever Colossus of the Colon, filing

the colon's deed in the courthouse of poetry's signature
punctuations early on (Dickinson owns the dash, O'Hara

the exclamation point, Cummings the parenthesis
and bracket, a stock account of influence and subsidy)

your mark languishing centuries as merely a pointer
"ok, here comes a LIST:"—until you staked a claim put meaning

behind it: again, and again: and again and again: "the quick
stop-and-go," the circle never closing, the rusty crank turning

the shelled butter bean planted, then harvested again, and again:
they who knew you claim you hated being pinned down

(scientific, living synthesis) and how you opened up the world's
tightening intellectual architecture, endless "what ifs" So, what if:

## Bag 3.

maybe the age demanded the colon: the chemistry of rot
equal parts building up and tearing down, a balanced equation

the seesaw of wedded actions, a barbell with round balls
on either extreme, win/lose, time split between the dugout and

hard against the warning path: like on Monday how I saw a huge
compost pit at the local college, a mound ten feet high, 4/5s

wood chips, grass trimmings, yard debris, and 1/5 cafeteria
food waste (corncobs, steak trimmings, wilted salad, napkins,

fried potatoes, soggy pizza crust) turned by a front-end loader
once a week, and when broken open with a pitchfork a million black

soldier fly larvae worked inside, like a business district of decay,
a street party of pulsing worms eating what we think of as trash

garbage, debris to be disappeared in landfills: the light is all
this world needs to thrive and be welcomed back into the living:

the small segmented maggots of the black soldier fly
a community, a growth industry, a division of our economy

over performing with unemployment at zero (birthed into labor
and grown strong on heavy lifting), and yet around us

the leaves are hauled away or burned, and the kitchen scraps
end up in the garbage or septic tank or ground and diluted

and flushed through sewers, and we pay not to see black
bags full of droppings, castings, shed skin, husks, tailings, trimmings,

cans, bottles, plastic bags, used baby diapers, hair, toenail clippings,
boxes, sheathings, caps, tampons, broken utensils, extra pills

(these more often flushed down toilets with ticks and condoms)
straws, Styrofoam cups (average useful life expectancy 15 minutes):

so, that list out of the way, let's get back to the end of the barbell,
the living, active end, the "I got up this morning and my vital signs

strong, so I'll get out of bed and try to write some poetry" end of
the human spectrum, and is this really that different than a single

black fly larvae about its work? Is making poetry out of observed
experience really that far afield from bacteria dissolving shit in

a composting toilet, or maggots chewing up a corncob in a pile of
wood chips (the iambic throb of cicadas in the background trees not

lost on anyone who pays attention to such cycles): that poetry is
compost is not an original idea, and if I were an academic I might

even have a footnote here (thank you Walt Whitman) to set
any reading mind in motion backward, which is not that unusual

a move since I've already brought Shelley and Byron into this
field of inquiry, and they've been dead and rotted for 200 years

(that is, except for Shelley's heart—Remember?—which Mary
Shelley wrapped in one of Shelley's poems and stored in a drawer

for 30 years before the shriveled organ, one of our greatest hearts
in the language, was finally buried in Dorsett, England): there

is no telling where this inquiry will end, and make fertile soil, as it could soldier on (like the fly) for pages more, or abruptly cease in

mid-sentence (Shelley's heart drowning) like an abandoned mine
shaft sent down into someone's claim that missed the mother lode

## Bag 4.

I have poured myself into this borrowed vessel, then stepped back
to see me overflow, as I have watched a liquid essence leave

the eyes of two dying dogs, and slip like a golden stream over the sides
and pool below in this memory only:

## Bag 5.

the Dixie Hummingbirds in town to sing one final time before
Ira Tucker died and driving around Spartanburg Ira told a story

of this southern town in the 1930s: a melon plant
growing downtown and Ira watering it every day for a month

and the vine growing, like Jack in the beanstalk, long and huge
winding around the vacant Main Street lot, green leaves like a

fleur-de-lis thriving, spreading, taking light in and the green vine
along, and Ira's one melon increasing in size and ripening

until he finally comes to pick it and it was gone, just like that
and though Ira did not say stolen, that's what I understood

from the story: somehow I was implicated, though I was born
twenty years later, but being guilty I was determined not

to steal Ira's melon again, and so we worked hard
to put on a good show, though from the west came a huge

thunderstorm and washed out the last few numbers, including
the long-anticipated "Love Me Like a Rock": I tell this story

because this morning a ruby-throated hummingbird flew
from cardinal flower to coreopsis, and there was the hoot owl's

single note in these particular woods, and the sun, late today
and there is no sign that it will disappoint the high expectations

of morning, though Earth's clocks are always trustworthy
and a squirrel has succeeded in his endless backyard plot to clear

the feeder, and morning's arrival has prolonged a few minutes
into light, and several aqua-tailed lizards are awake along the wall

and dark rocks line the flower bed, grottoes holding the short lives
of the cold-blooded and naturally blue: long lives are a blessing

among the caterpillars, broad-headed skinks, and the cardinal
with the red feathers vanished from his red head, and all

this seedbed of instances, each species a species of intent:
and yet I falter, remember two days ago the red-shouldered hawk

fly-ridden in the center lane and how it vanished overnight,
the road cleared by fox or coyote, carted off to feed the pups:

this day and yes the poem ends (you guessed it) with
a storm and rain, more inches piling up, almost ten

a month, yard a misplaced rain forest, and lightning
thunder moving through: now that we have Doppler (on both

devices—iPhone, iPad) we've started to worry more about
the trees, but sadly not in an ecological sense: instead

in a deductible sense: waterlogged lawns and houses
all over town this summer with trees fallen through

roofs, far beyond remembered lumber, and cracked rafters
2X6s long before the latest flora holocaust (hemlock, willow

oak, red bay): worry, yes, we pray the homeowner's prayer:
there's no silver lining in low premiums and the shit hits

the fan for everyone in their time, so give up, unless
you take a photo and through Photoshop paint a lining here

after the fact: back to the garden gauge, filled up three times
already this month, a silver lining for slugs and mosquitos

and me if we ever veer back to dryer seasons, but when would
that be? The Pleistocene's long gone, and if this place

ever looked like the Olduvai Gorge there's no sign of it now:
but seriously, this thing has to end, as all storms must:

bang/whimper/fizzle stick, or the last ball in the side pocket
the storm's on its last leg and our big oak still stands

sucker now for some future tree disease: Doppler shows Charlotte's
under a red watch, the Queen City, our neighbors to the east

I wouldn't turn my back on that tree though, since sometimes
we'll hear one will fall in the deep woods long after

the wind pushes through—it's a damn shame there is no law
especially gravity, can save us from our own surprises.

# Kingdom & Glory (2020)

—a long, sometimes historic poem about the Pacolet River
Flood of 1903

The impeded stream is the one that sings.

—Wendell Berry

## A Prologue

Ancient drainage forms a cleavage. The Great Atlantic Rift. What we now call continents—North America and Africa—moving apart at the rate your fingernails grow.

A region underlain with crystalline rock. Precambrian and Paleozoic. An eroding peneplain. Rapids along the rivers. Monadnocks. Low relief. Rolling knolls and rounded hillocks. Rivers, the active agents of erosion, from north to south, Hudson, Delaware, Schuylkill, Susquehanna, Potomac, Rappahannock, James, Roanoke, Haw, Yadkin, Pee Dee, Broad, Savannah, Chattahoochee, Coosa into Alabama.

And so the Pacolet, in the Broad River basin of the upper piedmont of South Carolina, which could be a French name of an early settler, or some say it could be a corrupted Cherokee word for "running horse," but maps say that the river was once, in the early 19th century, known as "The Sandy River," and the sand, laid down over eons, from the eroding backbone of the Blue Wall, still in each successive flood going back 250 million years.

Eternal cutbanks and sand bars. An alternating endless pattern of energy written on the land through deep time, like lines of this poem are written here.

And the people dropped like leaves in the not-so-long-ago time in this natural epic of water rising...

## Hoved Forth upon the Waters

Preacher Kingdom set his death grip on the belfry
in the rising flood. Kingdom's river-soaked Bible,
his only oar and lifeboat, sloshed upon the floor;
he, the Bible, and the church rode like pilgrims
on the current, and the one-room wood frame church
and walls did not come tumbling down
like Jericho; the meeting house held, and floated
more like the ark of old toward Union County.

Though Kingdom slept hard the night
before he woke to the smell of spilt kerosene; outside
the rain pounded like a tambourine on tin shack roofs;
but he'd heard that sound for days—not forty
like Noah's, but close as he'd ever come
in his lifetime; that oily smell pulled him from
the sleeping pallet and out the front door he saw
the run-away current already sluicing through
San-tuck's streets; a sheen like a fractured rainbow
caught the first light flowing; one alley away
the river bank sloughed like layer cake,
taking a company duplex with it; then Old Man Cox
swum out a splintered window in his nightshirt,
dragging his stunned wife Marie by her sleeve.

Preacher knew his calling, grabbed
his Bible, pushed open the church door, commenced
to ring the bell as warning to villagers
in the bottoms down below San-tuck; Kingdom
jerked the belfry rope with red raw palms; he yanked
so long he shed his night shirt from the sweat,
and the knot snapped lose from the rusted clapper;
Kingdom had to climb, but by the time he mounted

the belfry ladder, the last layer of red
mud bank peeled away and with one liquid pulse
picked up the church and dropped it in
the current wild between rows of mill shacks.

## Hymn of Hell on Earth

I see land sanded, shredded, sodomized
by water. No fire this time, only heaving
litanies of screaming doom—the paradise

of unbelievers washed, vile, a fiery lake
without the fire, wet sulfur smell.
Matthew's second death soaks us,

washed like lambs, the river people
that forgot, everlasting in our saturation.
Throw them in a washtub, and slosh.

Better to enter hell's hallway and sink
then float in sin high and dry.
Depart, depart—washed as you are

between two an indifferent cutbank
and the river's deep, forgotten bend.
Ride it out—stain salvation red.

## In Which Kingdom Seeks Refuge

All hell broke loose. Not hell exactly,
since hell is parched and full of sinners; this stream
brimmed with true believers, some washed that very
summer in the said-same river. From his vantage
Kingdom saw parked hacks and racks of kicking horses
swept downstream; he saw table-terraces of red clay
turn to pudding and dissolve; with gaping stare
he watched trolley tracks curled like so much
Christmas ribbon flush over where the dam used to be;
but Kingdom and his death-grip soon rode with them.

Preacher hurled a verse of rebuke
at the rising surge, "And I will establish my covenant
with you, neither shall all flesh be cut off any more
by the waters of a flood; neither shall there any more
be a flood to destroy the earth." From the floating
belfry Kingdom's sanctified voice boomed, the least
of the scattered congregants' worries.

The white plank church sloshed
side-to-side; the bell clanged and the river roiled; round
Kingdom more men and women floated out windows
of drowned mill houses all over San-tuck and swept
downstream in the building maelstrom. Some folks,
already drowned, floated feet-up and others still wide-faced
screamed Holy Christ! at the passing church and preacher,
then thrashed away into swamped eddies like water striders.

Kingdom thought his head would pop,
filled with the irregular ringing of the bell. Each sharp
clang and Preacher moaned, "I might just hurl my own
mortal coil into the muddy current and make for the nearest

shore," and then another clang renewed his faith
that, "the Lord had sent me up the steeple ladder at dawn
for good reason, and I should hang on until
the God Almighty changes his plans."

## Hymn of Buoyancy

I have been decried by sailing eddies,
shifted as eroded sand, fingers of loam
gyring in the ancient constricted floodways.

My flaxen hair-suit, my parchment,
drying lengthways by empirical sun, staggering
boat-wise now into this cubic wall of doom.

A church steeple of water preceeds me
and proceeds the way like a high altar
acolyte downtown, some Episcopal zeal,

or Methodist haughty copy of holiday ritual,
this watery body-double of spirit-land,
this rush of Pentecostal geomancy

etched instead by God's hands on water,
I surf into coves of delight and fear beyond
my spilt morning's coffee. Hold steady, Lord.

This is how your church should ride
the currents of a new century: full-bore the freshet,
false steps left on the inevitable sold-down shore.

## Admist the Infernal Freshet

But Preacher was no fool; he knew
his dire state, the church burping muddy water from
two windows now unshuttered in the ride; the old pine
planks creaked with each collision of wave and trough;
he knew the river bends would likely smash the House
of God to kindling never bound for any stove;
he prayed that instead of drown he'd cling to lumber
like a rat he saw pass, his only hope to come ashore
like Paul in his shipwreck.

Riding high above, Kingdom clutched his water-logged
Bible, reciting verses he remembered where water
was the rule; "From the west, people will fear the name
of the Lord, and from the rising of the sun, they will revere
his glory. For he will come like a pent-up flood that
the breath of the Lord drives along."

Kingdom craned his head upstream
but the west churned a watery hell; downstream the east
lit up like altar candles to shine him forth; in the morning light
Preacher could make out farm fields of inundated crops;
green stalks fired like sky rockets, and knots
of transfixed mill boys peering from far, flooded edges
of poor pastures, listened to the fast receding bell.

On the north ridge of the straightaway,
Kingdom watched two barefoot boys in overalls run along,
waving arms, following the church downstream; he hurtled
by like an evening train, and worse of all,
Kingdom soon reached the gorge below the village
where the river narrowed between two ridges, and he picked
up more hellish momentum;

As the church gained speed Kingdom saw terrified
cows and chickens and dogs pass by in the faster current
to either side, and he saw splintered store signs, porch gliders,
a lard bucket; he saw a man tangled in chicken wire,
a little boy calling from a raft of timbers, a naked man wearing
only an apron sprawled on a tree with the Devil's own black
snake in the limbs just below; he saw two women with cord
wood under their arms to stay afloat; he saw someone's
mail still bundled and tied with a red rag, and then,
as the church spun crazy in the current, he saw pushed
before it—a wooden kindling box, two uprooted cedar trees,
a line of rose bushes, the tube of a bicycle, and a canvas canoe
with two oars trailing, and a cotton bale bearing
one scrawny naked man.

"The Lord has cast his countenance upon you
and saved you from the daylose," yelled Kingdom
to the whirling wreck below.

"And left me adrift naked on this cotton bale?"
yelled the passenger. "What kind of crazy-ass God is that?"

## Hymn of the Once-Wild Land

Some god banished, probably Cherokee, with turkey
feathers for a beard, and a lanyard holding the severed
heads of three fence lizards, their mouths agape,

eyes still ajar, for they believe the world unfolds,
penitents to dawns, supplicants to even Eden's
diminishing 19th century shadow called

questionable; the Cherokee god finally sent
packing by a troupe of serious-mouthed Baptists,
Presbyterians, and one long strident exegesis

preformed from sweat-logged Bibles awash
on sawdust church floors, hymns of suffering,
hymns to wounds closed finally by mules,

(or so assumed the settled), hymns to land
furrowed and burned, hymns to peach trees
and the grunts and ambles of chinkapin pigs;

but now the fence lizard returns, riding high,
flood-born on a lumbered slab of oak panel,
a church wall, a tiny mote in a vanished god-eye.

## In Which Kingdom Performs His First Miracle

Preacher Kingdom tied a sloppy noose in the bell rope
and heaved it down toward the soaked rider on the bale.
He watched it sail like a floating strand in the wind off ripping
waves grown foamy in the morning's savage flood.

The pole-axed hitchhiker saw the rope,
grabbed it, looped his wrist, and the noose cinched down;
"Hold strong, pilgrim," Kingdom bellowed and hauled
the naked stranger toward the church's open yonder
window till the floater bumped like freight over battered
barrels, chicken coop boards, the row-boat, and swung
home-free in the window; landing in a pew, he slid
back and forth on the floor as the church geed and hawed
downstream.

No sooner did the lucky arrival clear the window
that the church snagged on some mysterious hidden stump
or cliff-rock in the Pacolet river bed and pivoted like a spun top,
throwing him back toward the window like a doll; the rope
still wrist affixed had acted like a slingshot and nearly pitched
him back in the drink. He caught the pane and hauled back in;
Kingdom flopped as well from one side of the belfry to the other,
then back to see the horror of the vacated cotton bale plunge
down the black throat of a outlying whirlpool and disappear,
a plug of tobacco down an avenging God's gulping throat,
then Kingdom knew that stow-away down below, a living message,
pulled from the river's craw and saved
like a praying fool among the hoving sanctuary of The Lord.

"Hordes of souls have marched to heaven
before thee," Kingdom sang, constricting a hymn to two verses,
"and let not one man, set free, doubt the believing power of His

grace." Inside the church the salvaged chosen one looked around.
There was no serenity in his refuge but at least the walls
held back the burping river in all but two windows
unshuttered in the flood; the swarth rider plucked the nightshirt
off the floor sloughed off by Kingdom in his heated ringing
of the bell before his climb; he slipped it on, fine as Joseph's
many-colored coat; now covered up,
the wayfarer held on and pondered his recent past;
that very morning he'd woke at home on Hill Street
and gazed down from what folks called Colored Town
and feared the rising river in the dawn;
he saw lights already on in the white man's mill,

"And your name shall be Glory,"
he said, and pulled on his ragged pants and gauzy shirt
and hauled ass to the closest shallows;
Glory looked out to where the rising surge had already taken
many wailing down the stream; some were clutching at branches
in the margins close enough to wade ashore, but others
were marooned like trash in rafted heaps of sheds
and Glory knew if he could ride a floating cotton bale
out he could haul them shoreward, and off he went;

Glory stuck his leg under twine
for purchase and paddled out with a picker stick;
he first coaxed a white man on the bale; the man stared
before he stirred, as if the archangel in face
had floated in to save him; "I went out to haul in 98 more,
for men and women were strung out like sopping
weeds in the water; then on the 100th trip a loose cottonwood
had rammed my bale and knocked me off; the current
ripped off my ragged clothes and left me naked
as baby Jesus in the manger; somehow I saved
himself and found another cotton bale to ride downstream
until I lodged before your church; I have no regrets

if indeed I do die here in this church, I've done all
I could to shuttle people to shore, using my cotton
bale like a lucky ark; praise Jesus, I'm loose and alive
on a froggy day," Glory bellowed to no one in particular;

Kingdom heard the lucky rider and opened up the crawlway
where the ladder mounted from below; "Come up, Glory,"
Kingdom said, "if we pass, we pass with a better view,
join me up above;" Glory heard the voice
of Kingdom pressing down, but did not budge; he liked it
where Glory knew the score, close to the water, though it seeped
in at every angle and sloshed about the pine-wood floor.

## Hymn to the Anadromous

Shadbushes burst forth
with white sentinel flags, the weeping
fish migration waits to proceed;

a dirge swallowed in the shallows
Trough Shoals, a harvest of travelers,
the Sixth Day's flippered and delivered

upstream eons between the calling
out of the Word and the receding now
clouds whipped into muddy cream

eddies roil like the last street car
from town, the seats are ledges
of gray inundated granite

something else travels
this reverse tide, the lily
wilted on the season's altar

decay, delay, depths of discount
sinners pay in this purgatory,
the last pageant of the resolved.

# Kingdom and Glory Garner Unlikely Fellowship from Shore

Kingdom, his acolyte sopped below, and his flotsam raft,
soon left the village nightmare and entered the lonely wilderness;
they outran the bodies of congregates, but the flooded river pressed
between hillocks and ridges and inundated forests and fields
and the surging water whispered in the submerged branches;
a mile downstream Kingdom began hearing voices.

He heard the dangling silky dogwoods speaking
in desperate sweet drawl; he thought he heard swamp oaks
keening, whistling a plea to join them as he passed...

The wild things pulled his mind ashore,
but running before the raft now the two mill boys seen
first below the gorge had parlayed a footpath through the bend
of the slowing river to their advantage—"Hay-o!" they cried
above the racket of the flood, no whispering silky dogwoods,
but brogan-footed boys bent on contacting the run-aways.

"Old man!" they yelled over slurping waters
and the steady grind of splintered beams, a floating cotton gin,
bedstead frames with still tucked tight-striped bedding
from a hundred emptied shacks buoyed downstream ready
for the sleepers, a wooden headboard, a mantel piece, a carved
spindle-leg table for a front room, a dozen floating storehouse
barrels emptied of nails, racks of flimsy curtains stained orange
and floating by like drowned barely glimpsed ghosts.

Along the shore debris caught in rafts—a pine tree,
limbs from someone's apple orchard, a metal beam that once
held the mill floor upright; when the boys' voices slipped

through misty air Glory answered with his own, "He ain't alone,
as I too have slipped the noose of the Devil's very hand
and stand a dripping supplicant before The Lord."

"Swim to shore, and we'll pull you in!" the boys yelled,
but the current, though spread out, had slowed little;
Kingdom watched trees and barrels dive and disappear,
only to explode back up and tap dance along the eddy's
wall and ping-pong back to the river's center;
the church held; maybe they were safe and soon headed
to high ground, to count the next day the Lords,
and themselves among the lucky who had met the deluge
and survived; but Kingdom's solace and sound conceit
of survival passed as the church bounced back
into the downstream current, no closer to shore than before;

Glory felt the lurch and looked out; he was full-face
forward against the eddy's outside standing wall, peppered
with a decoupage of lost households—a set of false teeth
chattered past, a half-full bottle of hair oil, the brush
from a woman's dresser, a toy giraffe with one leg splayed,
a baby doll soaked red with river water; a watch dog
still chained, his lip snarled in a death grip, a daily paper
tacked to a shack wall, the headline blurred,
a felt hat, shaped like a blooming tulip, a recipe for chicken
stew; the items all flowed past like a machine belt
as the church turned at took its place in the swirling current
tilted downstream by the lay of the land, for the stream
slightly downhill flow had turned gigantic in pumped
full of run-off from the miles between Clifton and Fingerville;

"We gone but not forgotten!" Glory yelled, his voice
receding; and the boys took off racing, a pasture before them
clear to the river's next bend, hunting the lost or escaped.

# Mired Amidst the Debris

Another mile and the Pacolet slowed precipitously;
the boys ran on, just in ear-shot, shouting out warnings
of what lay below; two hounds chased them as if they
ran a fox through the pastures still dry, shin-high
in corn; would Preacher Kingdom abandon his watchtower
and pitch his body in the drink and swim for shore?
He found comfort in the Word, "...though the waters rage
and foam..." but needed human comfort too; "Come up,
Glory," he yelled.

But Kingdom's bell and Kingdom's call were one,
so Glory did not climb; the noisy passenger below yelled back,
"You come down; I'm no faithful acolyte to fill my head with
the heartache of your bell, for so far it has not tolled for me."

From his window Glory appraised the river's riled
but slowing surface and calculated some obstruction below;
the church turned like a top offering him a view downstream,
and it was clear what lay ahead—

In Poole's Bend a wreckage dike had piled San-tuck's
debris from shore to shore, a dark mass, a tar baby stuck
with rough-hewn timbers, mill houses turned a kilter,
a tree lodged like a toothpick through the window of one,
and fire beset it all, and flames walked the splintered walls
like a dead ashy watchman, like God had too soon brought
his second answer ("...the fire next time...") down from heaven
before the first had yet subsided.

Where could the bobbing church lodge but amidst
this river-wreck? Where the flood took them, its slack current
still enough to settle floating spew against the wooden mire,

a two-story wrack-line, misery's high tide; they beached,
beam-to-beam against the swept-away company store.

By this time Kingdom saw the visage too; he scanned
the rubble up and down, looked for hope beyond the piles
of shattered cedar poles, the patina of rusted crumpled tin,
and fire leaped like spooked deer from house-to-house, shack-
to-shack, wreck-to-wreck, and from tower-height he saw
in the store the second floor ajar, mahogany counters piled
with glass broke out, like a wreck of box cars in the corner,
commerce derailed, spilling out white shirts and collars,
overalls, black boots, hat boxes, and then,
like some nightmare display, a dozen coffins laying
side-by-side, and a drowned corpse somehow splayed there.

The bell fell silent the first time since Kingdom climbed
to ring it raw with his own hands; now the sound was kindling
snap and crackle fire, and a nearby dog howling, then a single
woman's persistent nearby cry—"my baby, my baby, my baby!"

## Hymn for the Bottom Land

He made cowturds for His reasons,
made a valley smitten; He cleaved gneiss
bedrock, left a passage believers walked

all seasons but one—flood time, cloudburst,
storm months, gyres from the Gulf, downpours
above Lyman, Campobello, even Dark Corner.

He made reeds exalted; muskrats His raptures,
the V they push ahead in the water, His praise-tongue;
when the bobbing ducks work the shallows, He

tilts them back upright and makes scribbles
in the matted mud; flowing water worships
no God, but duckweed in the hydrosere?

Not rootless as a gypsy, His joke, primeval
on dry land; bur reed attends the shoals,
flats must make do with His muddy

overshoes, his planted poplar, ash, and swamp oaks;
the Cherokee sent a buzzard out, then the little water
strider, but His proof is leveed and alluvial.

## The Second Miracle

Effigies of heat streaked the sky, still robin-egg
blue from dawn; timber moaned, rubbed raw by the pressures
in the pile-up. Flood waters gurgled out the backside
of the dam. Matted household goods and stocks from the store,
pulverized pole barns, like a clutch of pick-up sticks, wobbly wood
sheds pressed into layered loaves with flattened trestles,
butchered boxcars, battered bridges, scraps of picket
fences and a thousand bobbing cotton bales; whole oaks,
poplars burn like matchsticks nail-struck on the watchman's nail—
dying mules moaned, sheep slept in hideous snatches
in their wool kickers, skewered by stray trolly rails.

The fire bucked and danced between kindling, wet
and dry; Kingdom leapt, scissor legged, onto what was soaked
and fire-proof, hop-scotching, dancing a nimble jig from rubble raft
to wickered roof to bobbing beam, until he reached the woman
resolute to save her baby—

But what Preacher saw sickened even the hardy
preacher's keen, a vision comfortable between heaven and earth—
dead bodies clutching last straws of hope, drowned
amidst the rubble, faces cast upward as if the Lord
had something else to say, some final word, some judgment
before the life passed over; then Kingdom followed the woman's
steady gaze and saw a living baby floating in a bread box surrounded
by fresh-baked bread, garlanded in the swirling current
by two buoyant cedar trees, all sailing forth toward a crevice,
the only open maw of leaking deadly flood
where it could go. Kingdom paused and did not move.
He stood like Lot looking back, lingered momentarily
on the path of fear and saw a vision city behind, burning
on the roiling river's rippled muddy plain.

"Yeah, was there ever a city of watery ruin like this great
flood of human misery set before us on this day?"
And then there came Glory, swaddled in firelight instead
of fear, riding on his cotton bale, snatching up the baby
box from the brush, paddling against the maw with his picker stick,
back toward the tilting church. "Lord, save us from our weaker
stages and too much prayer,"
Preacher, snatched the mother by the arm, hopscotched back across
the rubble toward the church,
"And give us strength like Glory for the miracles of the day."

# Fluvial Hymn

Sluice and gurgle, slosh, gush, gain
Heaven but lose the last bend of fertile field.
Dammed be the stomped uncle pole-axed

by the inundating fury of God, besotted
as any downstream first cousin, surprised
in the riverside duplex; dammed be the loom-

fixer now with no loom, only air,
the brick factory fallen in the roaring river
when righteous fury came to call!

The Holy math of destruction, sleeping
long in the Big Book—read it and weep—
a slumbering code, clicking muddy tumblers.

Your congregation now—catfish and penitent
mussels, holding fast to a sodden Golgotha.
Where are the choirs of riverine angels exalting?

He brings Holy Hell to those who forget!
The freshet freight train power of the Lord!
Abomination! Abomination! Abomination!

## Kingdom Takes on Another Hitchhiker

Step and straddle, then Kingdom paused and listened.
Had the church bell stopped ringing? Then the smoke broke
and there ahead it stood—wrapped now in muscadine vines
torn loose from riverside San-tuck groves; the steeple stood
garlanded with its crown of thorns.
Kingdom led his floundered
Mary forward by the hand, hop-scotching, straddling sinking rafts,
all moaning, all sodden, sucking at their feet and lives,
sinking in debris; if he could pause and ponder a backcountry
preacher could wring theology from such a scene—
but there was no time for that—he could not tarry—
Preacher asked, "Why stay here and die?"
Mary paused and would not jump. "No rebuke can make waters flee,
and not even buckets of prayer can tune this roiling
down into the mill pond you remember on calm Sundays."

Then he heard it once again, the bell. At least the bell
gave a song, a shape-note song against the blazing sky.

"Fear not," he said and took Mary by the hand and led her on—
But what a wasted hell they passed, jumping from floating
chest of drawers, to side-ways hog trough, to sideways
racket, the horses dead in harness—
Once Kingdom's foot
landed in a post office drawer amid sodden letters—a stew
of missives from far away, the blue ink bloomed and blotted
on each square.

Onward Kingdom and Mary hopped—the church
his stationary goal, a safe haven if only they could survive
the hop-scotch journey to its door. Onward, leap
and balance, step and straddle, Kingdom and Mary...

# Kingdom Breaks Free

Once Mary was in the door, Kingdom paused; Glory
held the baby in his arms; the smell of fresh bread filled the church
but could not drown the settled stench of burning flesh;
the debris dam blocked the river between two cliffs
but knitted in the pile-up of splintered settlement was a breech,
a roaring tunnel, a sucking maw, a draining tub,
as if the plug had been popped from above, and the river
ratcheting downstream; Preacher felt the church start to turn,
heard the bell overhead, at first a light metal clanging, followed
by the back-and-forth iron fracture of the air.

Spinning turned to gyre, and gyre to cyclometer;
"Hold on!" Kingdom yelled, and Glory, Mary, and her baby
clung to the rattling pews now lodged against the bare pine
walls; Kingdom climbed to the belfry where he could see—
smoke lay greasy on the water, but the steeple poked
a hole, rocking back and forth, the bell a nescience
Preacher could not halt; they spun like a top until sucked free.

Through the breech, the church bell announced
their descent; born again on the water's holy rolling, Kingdom
rocked on toward Union County.

# Hymn of Holy Hydrology

God owns tectonic uplift, and the devil,
downcutting; Cain's cutbank,
erosion's ark, Sodom's sedimentation.

Signify turbidity, earthly base-level change.
Signify the Lord's timely entrenchment.
Signify stream capture by His band of angels.

A view of the river: flooded channel, cut-off
meander, drowned bar. Distribution of discharge
in profane spaces—back forties, backlands,

and backwaters; heaven's hydro-geometry
is rise; God's velocity increases substantially
with gathered discharge (the dead rising),

the river's muddy width, the eddy spin.
Heaven is the suspended load. Heaven is slope.
Heaven is the mean annual flow, width, depth,

All this equals overflow, flood, little
hexes spayed upward on an X-Y axis,
shadows below a hatch of watery souls.

## Through Hell's Hallway

What felt like forty days Kingdom traveled downstream—
but at the speed of an Atlanta-bound freight: Nature's
scripture clears the stage, the players float chanting
"discharge, volume, peak" as the river seeks the sea.

The church held together. No miracle, physics
being what it is; a top spins, a Jew's dreidel wobbles only
at one end; the sky tightened above, the flooded banks
rushed past, the mill boys chased Kingdom impossibly
through the flooded corn fields, the lime-green stalks
knee-high a month before the $4^{th}$ of July;
Kingdom's head felt like a pumpkin hit with a baseball bat
every time the bell clanged; then on shore, as if summoned,
he saw flash past one of the mill boys pitching
a baseball to people floating down, rubble-riders,
trash-clingers, buoyant in the tide—the ball tied up
in string, a rope affixed to the free end; two men floated by.

"They mount up to the heavens, and they go down
again to the depths; Their souls melt because of trouble,"
Kingdom preached, and with no blessing the men made
the river's middle where deep currents flushed on downstream,
past the shore's detritus and then they dove like feeding ducks.

But the dark was also paradise; kingdom saw flashing
by on the river's flush June sides, the swamp milkweed blooming,
blue *lobelia*, the spotted touch-me-nots, black willows.

# Hymn of Drowned Souls Rising

Let me dry heave in heaven.
Let my lungs drain on its shore.
Let my rough linen jumper stiffen in paradise.

Because of the fragrance of burning tar
in the swamped commissary,
your name is acrid until we steal away.

Let my bare feet swell again in sunshine.
Let my shriveled toes puff up in his Glory Hole.
Let the leaves matted in my hair be wondrous.

## The Precious Cargo Rides Onward

A straight shot, like the blast of a .410
down an alleyway of post oaks squirrel hunting
on his daddy's farm, Kingdom rode to Union County;
the church spun slow and Kingdom climbed down
from his belfry perch; he spied Glory drained
from every inch, sodden with the tide of his deeds;
he spotted Mary tending her baby on a pew;
"Surely, I have calmed and quieted my soul,
like a weaned child with her mother is my soul with me,"
Kingdom spoke and crumpled in a corner.

# Hymn of Meanness

Grows like a wart in the out-of-the-way.
Mushrooms in the wet crannies.
Runs the rivers, knocking heads.

Killed a dog, and then another.
No reason. Needs only spite to cross.
You looking at me? You don't like it?

You think I give a damn?
Would go back from where it came
if the road wasn't flooded.

## Trouble Ahead, Kingdom Finally Gets Everyone Ashore

Across the flooded river Kingdom saw the mob;
they tracked the grounded church, high-stepping
through chinquipin thickets on the other shore; slouch-hat
country codgers with shotguns, blunderbusses, drop breech
squirrel rifles, Burnside carbines, bolt-actions, Baby Dragoons,
tarnished Enfield rifle-muskets left over from the War;
they yelled and cussed and pointed over the river's
muddy roaring maw at Kingdom and his ragged pilgrim band
from upstream; foreigners from further than you could walk,
Bathshebas and Beelzebubs from beyond the nearest ridge;
the salt on Glory's skin shined in the sun, dried to patchy
whiteness stepping into the heat, like scabs of talcum
peppered from above; they knew not what else Kingdom
might have within his sanctuary walls;

Hours passed and on they trundled in the flood;
Kingdom slept and nearly drowned from the seepage
at every tilt; and then he stood with a start when
the church heaved up hard on something solid
in its path against its fate; living privet poked in through
a busted window and Kingdom knew they'd lodged
in another dam, waiting to be flushed into the maw again
like a top; but he looked out—the shore was right aside,
dry land beckoned; the ark of new had finally come to rest.

"We here," Glory intoned.

# 25 Dream Ghazals (2022)

“Intellect takes you to the door, but it doesn’t take you into the houses.”

—Shams Tabrizi

## I

I dream of house maintenance and a gift
of a comforter, maybe a signal of love to come.

Listless battles, news map monitored for movement.
Foreign hemorrhages. Borders. Brigades of uncertainty.

Intermediate attention is on my health, stable as dominoes.
Long-term prognosis: sucks, like everyone else.

In the hills a friend talks of all Dark Corners, places
where the edges collide, all hotly contested, never settled.

Pantries are for storage, not concealment. Or both?
I jimmy the doors one by one. Meal moths flutter out.

## II

The rancher talks of growing grass in a greenhouse
the size of a basement and abandoning pastures forever.

Missiles are back in the news and the ideologies of czars.
I thought we were over the past. Silly us.

If the dog pisses on the couch again, that's it.
The cushions smell like the wards of old men like me.

Birds at dawn. A dinosaur chorus. Hope or last hurrah?
A comet pokes through the clouds. Disaster is always overcast.

In a decade the invading tanks will serve as planters or scrap
the Chinese melt down, more likely. Girders are the future.

Gas is five dollars a gallon, but the Cretaceous
was always expensive. Ask any petroleum geologist or dreamer.

## III

The dog is circling again. I smell shit everywhere,
even under the couch where it's dark.

As the numbers tick upward I worry about
the future. Now, the present is its own dire numerology.

The kite I've chosen, the blue and white one,
can't stay up forever. It too will fall to earth.

Even eating in a restaurant, I don't get
what I want. Then it occurs to me meat is an option.

Should I take a gift to someone? Wrapped in colored
paper and so obviously a spoon? Or choose a square box?

We are sitting in a pickup in the near woods.
They'd shot a female manikin's crotch full of holes.

We're back home. Travel is never existential
as long as there are corridors of escape.

The dryer sounds like gunfire.
No, the dryer sounds like crickets in a can.

## IV

They're going to write about this point
in history. Not about any of us here.

This feels dangerously unthought.
This feels like freedom, protested or otherwise.

I'm in an office and suddenly my mouth
is bleeding. My front tooth is loose and bloody.

Then I'm a poet sitting on a mountain top
throwing down chunks of shale.

Wild animals are in the yard, an owl
and her fledgling, a bear and her cub.

Cutting grass at the Country Club they found me.
They lashed me to the mower with my own belt.

Vocation and avocation sometimes merge.
Reading and writing disappear those days.

The surgeon says, my neurons really fire
when I get my hands on a knife.

V

The window strike didn't kill the cardinal.
A broken heart did. Who put a house there?

His neighborhood has a park renovated into a preserve.
You'd think the professor would become a naturalist.

He's still a little boy with his thumb
in his mouth. God bless him.

Here is what poetry is really all about—
The flaunting of the seven deadly sins.

I walk down the long hall and into the bathroom.
I say, I really want a house.

There's a stereo in the living room. A chair.
It's a nice stereo. I'm hoping the owners don't come back.

When I dream I'm an old man
the front yard is always full of coyotes.

## VI

A wounded lion is transformed into a jaguar,
chased down by two hounds.

People's faces—I'm guilty and immature.
Besides, the good news is that everything is haunted.

In terse broken English the editor explains
the source interviews the place in your pages.

I have never told you, but it has always meant
a great deal we connected.

We all have our delusions. We believe.
Democracy has more capacity for pain.

From an epigraph: All imaginary animals
are monsters and wonders, deflecting and absorbing.

At the intersection of Hemingway Highway
and Cowhead Road you can find the best pork.

On a plane are a donkey, an alligator,
and a dog. A family explains they're used to flying.

## VII

The house on CNN with the top floor
burned off. Is that his capacity for chaos?

Who could not draw lessons from collapse?
A kingdom of demagogues and behind that, big money.

The arsonist doesn't have a plan.
The arsonist is happy with the flames.

Ideology is always corrupt. Ideology is not
gospel. It's a repeated script.

He thought I gave the Chinese a pass
because they'd pulled billions out of poverty.

But that's the genius of what is ours—
a consensus always competing with autocracy.

## VIII

This month the dog turns fifteen. I'll buy him
a T-bone and not worry about the consequences.

Your dad is sitting on a stud wall
talking about what went wrong with the house.

There are hundreds of hours of audio tapes
of my mother and you give them to me for my birthday.

I'm in a little study plot in the Preserve.
There's an old rock wall and a pit for cooking a pig.

The poet's hair is beyond white. It's crystal.
He looks like a cherub. But I know better.

There's a donkey I'm unloading.
I operate him by way of my truck entry fob.

I'm way disorganized and I know it.
We're holed up in the house, waiting for the invasion.

## IX

I moved through the middle-wood with
confidence. Most frightening was midmorning.

In the fireplace the mortar is falling out.
The light shines through. The blocks have shifted.

Four new toilets wait on a pallet in the drive. You say,
"We'll get twenty good years. You'll be 87 and me, 84."

The creek is high and muddy. Storms
default to clearer skies and trailing clouds.

It was a great day. Several email exchanges about
translation and literary ripples on the surface.

It felt like healthy rats were sliding in toboggans.
Like I'd been delivered somewhere.

Like I was forced to watch a lamb hunt.
I swear, "You idiots, they're lambs not coyotes."

## X

On the coldest days the songbirds drain the feeder.
But on the warmest they do the same.

Paddling on a lake I often cross open water
when I probably should hug the shore.

I hear voices coming from dark places, a closet,
or an open door with no light.

We are holed up in the house, waiting for the invasion.
The land troops will arrive first.

We have rifles we don't fire.
They have rifles too and aren't so shy.

How will I explain the snarl of confusing
highways in the middle of the journey?

In a hundred years titmice will still be here.
What species will push north?

Facts and particulars. No softened generalities.
Build these up the way a house rises, stud by stud.

## XI

What would you tell the you that was here
before this? Or the one before that?

The surgeon said what I had was unusual.
He said he'd never seen it in 400 patients.

I read the latest *tabula rasa*. I have the presence
of mind to continue. I can start the baby aspirin.

We have moved away from direct cultivation,
even though the endless grasslands are vanishing.

Change of scale is a good thing. Hope breaks
the shell like the beak of a baby bird.

# XII

In deep lyric grieving often narrative returns.
I go to the cemetery to look for a particular stone.

In times like this I want to be a bat, not a human.
I want to be here, to dig clay, to make pottery.

The trees and animals all spin together.
Is writing a total waste of time?

Last month all I had was forty pages of notes,
snowflakes, and blooming annuals in the yard.

The poet said he learned total arrogance with no
support system. Look at him now. Dead as a doornail.

## XIII

She's ready to blow apart at any instant.
Grief? I've had to be more patient.

We travel not only for escape. Novelty
doesn't announce itself. It arrives.

A butterfly flies into my heart.
What is my own evaporates.

Sleeping on a mattress in the front yard
we are so comfortable we forget our plans.

A poet with a small shaved head and flowing
body holds court at the drugstore.

I show him the bird blind but a fireman
tells me it's too close to the waterfall.

I wake up deep in the night
in a panic about our boats.

Well, there's more to it than that,
he says. There's your mother.

## XIV

At the wild end we remember dreams
not data, the dead poet reminds me.

Warm for over a week and the Weather Service
calls it anti-winter.

The dog came home from the kennel
unable to walk. We'll nurse him along.

The political divide corresponds to free
and slave states like before the Civil War.

A vast and powerful anger. Another thought:
Don't Look Up. I believe it's all very real.

There will be large marine and terrestrial
extinctions. It's all a garden now.

Maybe someday I will be converted or
promoted. They'll teach me something new.

## XV

If all this takes off, we could be upended
again. It's just a matter of time.

Like John Clare, I would like it said
that I witnessed it all from ground level.

The vet's put the dog on gabapentin.
He can't climb stairs now.

It doesn't take a poet to realize imagination
is the absence of imagination.

The dark isn't astronomy.
Light isn't always light either.

## XVI

Poetry's mandate is to measure—
the year's rhythm, the bloody heartbeat.

So much opinion about place.
My take on the world is we're all doomed.

In the mountains we hiked to Black Balsam.
On the way back we stopped in Tinsel Town.

Trying to right myself—a soul-
wrenching effort. To find out who I am.

I am still looking for grace and poise.
I am still looking for what works.

We no longer seem to be sailing.
This long passage ends in the grand questions.

I've been making images of spring tides.
The water here is not enough to sustain.

## XVII

A day of storms is over. Deadfall.
Mud that might just freeze.

What does it really mean to be freed up?
That never had a conscious hold on me.

I've walked every day. Just circling.
I even saw seventeen deer in two groups.

There will be plenty of time to rest.
Stay in eternal motion.

The lesson: the distribution of outcomes
is never certain. Never fair.

The calculus of grief is cruel. Shoot
shotgun prayers. Hope to hit something.

## XVIII

Look for a little while into what's
long abandoned, waiting as part of the work.

At first we just talk. Then she looks at me
and says, you are the one.

The limbs are bare, the strings tangled,
but we manage to keep them from breaking.

On a beach road we stop
for the box turtle. Birds in the sky, far off.

Floods. Two canoes. No one seems
to be hunting. Canoes everywhere.

We go on a bus. We stay one night
then everyone leaves without me.

It's true, I say, my mother
lost her teeth at twenty-five.

Don't turn on me. Run around the block.
I'll hunker forever in the dark city.

## XIX

The blood has stopped, but the tooth
is loose. I go shower off the blood.

My reading is both concentrated and scattered.
I particularly like *The Howl of Disgust*.

The locker is too small for my clothes.
I've broken several appointments with the past.

What about the word left blank
In the third stanza?

I can only imagine what it's like over on Twitter.
Do I need twenty-two books on Joseph Campbell?

We met on the patio. The weather
was perfect for drinks and snacks.

It made me sad that I'm not more invested.
What is possible? Colonizing and consuming?

## XX

I like uniforms better than costumes.
The biggest obstacles are political.

The poet always feels foreboding.
The future can't please everyone.

I have the wrong helmet on.
He's explained the offense but I'm struggling.

Simple notions clear us of our ancestors.
I planted honeysuckle and peeled the apples.

Now it's harder to communicate
and I feel the loss.

Home has acquired a frayed edge. After all,
it's not the dog sleeping on the couch.

My feeling has always been language
was more than sufficient.

I saw him often and knew
he was settled in the small house.

What does poetry know?
I'll come back to that at some point.

## XXI

The rain's falling and I'm listening
to a podcast called *No World Order*.

The kitchen is burned and also under
the bed. This is where I live.

There's a small book about a girl.
I remember the tactile feeling.

She's standing outside, right beside
me. She's ready to come over.

I like the kitchen,
but what about the guard dogs?

Her hair is not black.
It's not cut into a perfect bowl.

There's a pulse of language,
but no words. It's all narrative.

There is no need for it anymore
as long as the voice is speaking.

## XXII

There are magic objects all around.
There's a parachute in a drawer.

We are falling—in harness—
all floating down.

White asters still bloom in patches
along the trail between the bridges.

The backdoor latch clicks
and the dog falls back asleep.

I'm on a hill, pushing a vacuum cleaner.
I'm cleaning the street.

Laser lights of air defense in the night sky.
This isn't a war of reporting.

Mechanics fare better than romantics
because they don't fear machines.

Poets are an isolated lot—
talking only to each other, self-centered.

The others are mostly in suits.
Maybe I don't love enough.

## XXIII

You've got to admire him. He's a man
with a complete system, no matter how wrong.

Sweeping vistas, salt air, and gulls,
pinned down by gunfire.

Exile? Is that the answer?
The shape is all wrong, so we go at it with sheers.

Time has a strange way of constellating
itself if you just watch.

So much rain. Dead pond turtles
all along the road.

The shattered bodies of honeybees
stuck in the wipers.

## XXIV

It's not that he didn't
enjoy a good story. He loved story.

Temperamentally he was prepared
to be scientific or genealogical.

We split a plate—blood sausages,
avocado, a fried egg, and rice.

The sign said simply, anything helps.
Later, we stopped for gas and beer.

A one-eyed dog was on a trailer.
He seemed to be very appreciative.

What will rural America look like
in fifty years? A slow bleed.

## XXV

I'm afraid to look down, backwards,
or forward. The path is only wide enough for an ox.

I'm reading a manuscript to my family.
The river is low, and it's been that way all summer.

I take out a handkerchief and unwrap
a purple spotted bulldog.

I tell them a story, like a koan.
"Now, think about that for awhile."

# End Notes and Acknowledgments

**"FROM THE THREE KINGDOMS" (1980)**

"From the Three Kingdoms" was written in a rental house in Charlottesville, Virginia. I have nodded toward Ezra Pound and Gary Snyder as antecedents to this poem. Thanks to them, and to Gregory Orr, for his poems and for reading it in early versions. And also, to David Lee for his long poems and for encouragement, and to D. E. Steward for early mentoring in the ambition of the long poem. The preface was published in *The Mickle Street Review.*

**"AGAINST INFORMATION" (1995)**

This long poem was written in the first house I ever owned, on McDowell Street, a block from Wofford College, in Spartanburg, SC. The poem was written in a period of daily morning writing (that I called "poetry pushups") inspired by William Stafford's composition methods, but William Blake and Allen Ginsberg were the true twin godfathers of the composition. Blake's footprints and spirit are everywhere. As for Ginsberg, I saw his "Howl" as what the "age demanded" back in the 1950s. It was my hope "Against Information" would speak to some of the anxieties of the early 1990s. It seems to have happened. This poem is the only one of this group that was fully published, appearing in the central position of my collection *Against Information & Other Poems* (New Native Press, 1995). There also was a video with a Spartanburg premier by filmmaker Michael Ferguson, a multi-media performance in Asheville (with musician Greg Olson) recorded and released as a cassette tape by New Native Press. The reviews of the book were numerous. The concluding section of *Against Information*, "Certainty," appeared in *The Asheville Poetry Review* (1995). *Point* (Columbia, SC) printed the entire poem *Against Information* (1994.) New Native Press printed a limited edition multifold broadside of the entire poem (May 1994) before the book was released in 1995.

**"TWEET" (2013)**

This poem was written a decade after I married Betsy Teter, and by then we had built our house on Tempo Court and on Lawson's Fork Creek in Spartanburg, SC. Twenty years after the success of "Against Information" Thomas Rain Crowe, my publisher at New Native Press, wrote and asked me if I would write a new response to the Information Age, which had swept over us all like a tidal wave.

I had not stayed technologically pure. I bought my first cell phone in 2007, so I did not wade into "the Information Age." I immersed full body. The poem was written on the screened porch in the notes function of my iPhone, as would be much of my work from that point on. "Tweet" was what I came up with—the three-line stanzas because that fit the space on the iPhone screen (much like Archie Ammons with his adding machine tape) in direct contrast to the "verse paragraphs" of "Against Information."

"Tweet" is a direct result of Thomas Crowe's poetic challenge and the personal challenge of reflecting on the app called "I-Bird Pro" and birding from my screened porch. By 2010 I had maybe my fourth or fifth generation "smart phone." The jury is still out on how smart they are.

Two Sections from "Tweet: A Long Poem," appeared in the anthology *Mountains Piled upon Mountains: Appalachian Nature Writing in the Anthropocene* edited by Jessica Cory (West Virginia University Press, 2019).

**"LANDFILL THIS—FIVE BAGS OF GARBAGE FOR ARCHIE AMMONS" (2014)**

I began to work on this poem on my screened porch on Tempo Court about the same time I was writing "Tweet." I had read A. R. Ammons' long poem *Garbage* many times. I wrote "Landfill This" as a contemporary response to *Garbage*. The long-lined couplets and several other stylistic tics echo Ammon's original poem. The content is often environmental though at times it's literary-historical and contemporary pop culture as well.

This poem appeared in *Anthropocene Blues* (Mercer Univer-sity Press, 2017) broken up into sections, scattered throughout the book, and retitled "Erosion." Ray McManus is responsible for that suggestion.

**"KINGDOM & GLORY" (2020)**

Written on Tempo Court in Spartanburg. Originally "Kingdom & Glory" was titled "Trouble the Waters." The earliest draft I have dates to 2014 though it was not finished until the next decade. The origins of this poem can be found in my reading of Robinson Jeffers' long poem *Cawdor*. I love Robinson Jeffers well beyond my ability to explain. He confirms for me the idea that certain poets, though they are often disappeared or dissolved in the group minds of poetry institutions, can be out there multiplying in their usefulness to individual poets anyway.

Jeffers' characters suffer from oversized tragic flaws. The men and women in his long narrative poems have as much in common with Oedipus and Electra as they do my neighbors. Like the characters in Greek tragedies, their dramas grow out of murder, incest, and wrath, not merely boundary disputes and covenant violations.

I knew if I wanted the long poem to work, I needed memorable characters. Kingdom came from reading about a real church washed into the floodwaters and surviving intact for many miles downstream. I tried to imagine the preacher and Kingdom came to be. Glory? I needed someone for Kingdom to talk to.

Though the flood in this poem and its characters came from my imagination, there was a real Pacolet River flood on June 6, 1903. It's documented quite fully in newspaper accounts, many of which I read and borrowed from. This poem is dedicated to the people of Clifton and Pacolet who died that day. G. C. Waldrop read and commented on this poem at several stages. Thanks to him for that. "Hymn for the Bottomland" appeared in *Tar River Poetry* in 2017.

**"25 DREAM GHAZALS" (2022)**

The ghazal is an old Persian poetic form and has been adopted by many practitioners through the centuries. It is often considered a strict metric form, but many (and I am one) do not adhere to those conventions. What many take from the tradition is a minimum of five free-verse couplets, not related by logic. The only thing often giving the poem coherence and meaning is a metaphoric leap from couplet to couplet. I wrote these ghazals in a time of distant war and nearby personal grief. The ghazal couplets were mined from whatever floated through the inner shoals of my imagination over a single month in early 2022. Many, but not all, of the images come directly from an old dream journal I have kept for forty-five years. I was reminded by the composition of each poem what Freud said: that the unconscious has no time clock.

An edition of "50 Dream Ghazals" pamphlets was produced in the spring of 2022 and mailed to friends.

## The Author

John Lane is the author of many books of poetry and prose. He has won the Louisville Review Prize and Prairie Schooner's Glenna Luschei Award.

His ABANDONED QUARRY: NEW & SELECTED POEMS won the SIBA (Southeastern Independent Booksellers Alliance) Poetry Book of the Year prize in 2012. A co-founder of the Hub City Writers Project in Spartanburg, SC, Lane also taught creative writing and environmental studies at Wofford College for over three decades.

In 2014 he was inducted into the SC Academy of Authors and his literary papers are part of The Sowell Family Collection in Literature, Community and the Natural World at Texas Tech University.